Wrigley Hits 100

A Celebration of the Cubbies, Chicagoland,
and the Best Baseball Field in America

JOHN SNYDER

CLERISY PRESS

Most of this work is derived from the author's previously published work, *365 Oddball Days in Chicago Cubs History* (Clerisy Press, 2010).

For further information, contact the publisher at:

Clerisy Press
306 Greenup Street
Covington, KY 41011
clerisypress.com

ISBN 978-1-57860-557-6; eISBN 978-1-57860-558-3

Edited by Jack Heffron

Cover and interior designed by Scott McGrew

Cover photo by By Giants27 (Own work)
   [CC-BY-SA-3.0 (http://creativecommons.org/licenses/by-sa/3.0) or
   GFDL (http://www.gnu.org/copyleft/fdl.html)], via Wikimedia Commons

Interior photo by Rdikeman at the English language Wikipedia
   [GFDL (http://www.gnu.org/copyleft/fdl.html) or CC-BY-SA-3.0
   (http://creativecommons.org/licenses/by-sa/3.0/)], via Wikimedia Commons

Distributed by Publishers Group West

Happy Birthday, Wrigley!

The Addison stop on the Chicago L carries visitors and residents to one of the most beloved stadiums in America: Wrigley Field. Many sports fans contend that no city loves its athletic teams more than the Windy City, and as that is arguably true, Wrigley is the heart for Chicago's body (complete with big shoulders—thank you, Carl Sandburg) and soul.

Built in 1914 as Weeghman Park for the Chicago Whales, Wrigley has served as the home field for the Chicago Cubs since 1916. It was also the home of the Chicago Bears from 1921 to 1970. As with a number of early NFL franchises, the Bears (originally the Staleys) changed their team name to reflect the longer-term tenant: Bears . . . Cubs . . . get it? While most Chicago fans remember the Bears playing at Wrigley, it's still a surprise that the Monsters of the Midway were ensconced there for five decades. More eyebrow-raising is the fact that the Bears won way more championships (including four at Wrigley) than the Cubs (zero) in the last century.

Wrigley Field is the oldest ballpark in the National League and is second only to Fenway Park in Boston as the oldest active ball field in the majors. It's known for its human-powered scoreboard, its ivy-covered brick outfield wall, the nasty and unpredictable winds coming off Lake Michigan that play havoc with fly balls, and its status as the last major league park to have night baseball.

Winner of the SABR Baseball Research Award, author John Snyder digs deep into the Wrigley archive to give readers a daily dose of titillating tales and trivia. Each page brings a couple of new stories—whether it's a happy birthday to a colorful Cub or an "on this day" slice of history or a question that only the most serious Wrigley diehards will be able to answer.

This compendium of facts and stories is an affectionate portrait of a ballpark that has earned landmark status as one of the best in the nation. Wrigley has been the site of as many broken hearts as broken bats, but every spring—to turn a phrase on that word—hope again springs eternal.

Happy birthday, Wrigley. We love you!

January

January

On this date in 2009 . . .

The Chicago Blackhawks laced up their skates and played the Detroit Red Wings in the 2009 Winter Classic, the National Hockey League's annual throwback/outdoor game. The Hawks versus the Wings is certainly one of the oldest and most fierce rivalries in professional hockey, even when played in "The Friendly Confines"—Ernie Banks's nickname for Wrigley during his Hall of Fame career there. The rink ran across the baseball field from third base to first base, which means that the puck was dropped for the opening face-off in the near vicinity of second base. The Red Wings won 6–4.

Wrigley has also hosted full seasons of college sports (notably teams representing DePaul and Northwestern Universities), professional soccer (the other kind of *futbol*), and numerous rock concerts. Wrigley's neighbors don't take as kindly to loud music as they do victory celebrations, though truth be told it's been so long since a sports championship has been won at Wrigley that the two kinds of "parties" have never really overlapped . . . so it's hard to say for sure.

January

Happy Birthday Bill Madlock.

A four-time National League batting champion, Madlock was born on January 2, 1951, in Memphis, Tennessee. He led the NL twice with the Cubs, hitting .354 in 1975 and .339 in 1976. Madlock won his second title on the final day of the season, with four hits in four at-bats during an 8-2 win over the Expos at Wrigley Field. Going into the contest, Reds outfielder Ken Griffey, Sr. led Madlock .337 to .333. Cincinnati manager Sparky Anderson kept Griffey out of the game against the Braves at Riverfront Stadium to preserve his lead in the batting race. To pass Griffey, Madlock needed four hits in a maximum of five at-bats. In the first inning, Madlock laid down a perfect bunt for a hit. In the second, he beat out a roller down the third base line. Madlock's third plate appearance came in the fourth inning, and he delivered a single into right field. He now trailed Griffey .3375 to .3372. Madlock took the lead when he laced a single into left in the sixth. Griffey was now the pursuer, and Anderson hustled him into the game in Cincinnati as a pinch hitter. Griffey struck out, remained in the contest, and was retired again. Cubs skipper Jim Marshall lifted Madlock for a pinch hitter in the eighth. Madlock finished the season with a .339 batting average, while Griffey ended up at .336.

The question of the day.

Who is the only Cubs pitcher since 1930 to win as many as 24 games in a season?

Larry Jackson won 24 in 1964 with a record of 24-11 on a Cubs team that was 76-86. Jackson came to Chicago in a trade with the Cardinals on October 11, 1962. He was 31 years old and had a lifetime record of 101-86. Jackson's best season in St. Louis was in 1960 when he was 18-13, and his 282 innings led the National League. With the Cubs in 1963, he had a 2.55 ERA in 275 innings on a club that was 82-80, but Jackson received miserable batting support and posted a won-lost ledger of only 14-18. In 1964, his ERA rose to 3.14, but the Cubs hit well when he was on the mound, leading to his 24-11 mark. The only other 20-game winners in the NL that season were Juan Marichal (21) and Ray Sadecki (20). The success was short-lived, however, as Jackson became the rare pitcher to follow a 20-win season with a 20-loss season, with a 14-21 record in 1965. The Cubs traded him to the Phillies on April 21, 1966, in a deal that netted the Cubs Ferguson Jenkins. Despite his 24-11 season, Jackson was 52-52 as a Cub. After his playing days, Jackson served four terms in the Idaho House of Representatives.

The question of the day.

Who holds the major league record for consecutive games with an RBI?

First baseman Ray Grimes of the Cubs holds the record with 17 from June 27 through July 23, 1922. During the record-breaking, 17-game streak, Grimes drove in 27 runs and had 29 hits in 67 at-bats for an average of .433. He also registered seven doubles, three triples and three home runs. Between games 10 and 11 of the streak, Grimes was out of the lineup for 10 days because of a back injury. During the 1922 season, he hit .354 with 99 RBIs, 45 doubles and 14 homers. Grimes was 28 years old, and it looked as if he might have a long and prosperous career. Unfortunately, his back problems flared again in 1923, and he was never able to play regularly or productively. The closest anyone has come to breaking Grimes' record since 1922 is Mike Piazza, who had an RBI in 15 straight games with the Mets in 2000. No other Cubs batter has an RBI streak longer than 11 games. Grimes's twin brother, Roy, also played briefly in the majors in 1920. Ray's son, Ray, Jr., was a big leaguer with three clubs from 1938 through 1946.

05 January

Happy Birthday Riggs Stephenson.

Stephenson was born on this date in Akron, Alabama, in 1889. He played for the Cubs as an outfielder from 1926 through 1934 and compiled a batting average of .336, the highest by any player in club history with at least 2,000 at-bats. His lifetime on-base percentage of .408 is second only to Hack Wilson's .412. Stephenson and Wilson were Chicago teammates and played alongside one another in the outfield from 1926 through 1931. Stephenson was 28 years old when the Cubs acquired him from Kansas City, an American Association team. Previously, he played five seasons with the Cleveland Indians, mostly as a second baseman, but a shoulder injury suffered while playing football at the University of Alabama limited his throwing ability. Cleveland sent him back to the minors despite hitting .337 for them. Stephenson's career .336 batting average ranks 19th all-time by players with at least 4,000 plate appearances. No player since 1900 with a higher average has been denied election to the Hall of Fame. Stephenson's relatively short career, lack in hitting power and below-average defensive play have prevented him from receiving a plaque in Cooperstown. He only played 1,310 games in his career and hit just 63 home runs.

06 January

Happy Birthday Lee Walls.

Lee Walls, who played for the Cubs in the outfield from 1957 through 1959, was born on this date in 1933. He gave Cubs' fans an unexpected treat on April 24, 1958, with a three-home run game during a 15-2 win over the Dodgers at Memorial Coliseum in Los Angeles. Walls also drove in eight runs. He collected a two-run homer off Don Drysdale in the first inning, a three-run shot against Roger Craig in the fifth and another three-run homer facing Ron Negray in the seventh. All three were popped over 40-feet high above the left-field fence, which at the foul pole was only 257 feet from home plate. It was only the fifth major league game ever played in Los Angeles. The winning pitcher was Gene Fodge, in what would be the only victory of his career. Heading into the 1958 season, the bespectacled Walls was 25 and had 19 homers in 942 career at-bats. He clubbed nine home runs in a nine-game span from April 23 through May 1 in 1958. Walls finished the season with 24 homers and a .304 batting average. He was not able to sustain his success, however, and never hit more than eight home runs in any season after 1958.

The question of the day.

What is the most number of runs scored by the Cubs on Opening Day?

The Cubs' record for runs scored in the first game of the season is 16, and it was accomplished in back-to-back seasons. On April 4, 2005, the Cubs collected 23 hits and thrashed the Diamondbacks 16-6 in Phoenix. Derrek Lee had four hits, including two doubles and a homer. He also drove in five runs. Aramis Ramirez picked up a home run, a double and a single in four at-bats, in addition to scoring four runs and driving in four RBIs. Todd Walker and Jeromy Burnitz each banged out three hits. The game was Burnitz's first with the Cubs. On April 3, 2006, the Cubs again scored 16 runs in the opener with a 16-7 victory over the Reds in Cincinnati after President George W. Bush threw out the ceremonial first pitch. Matt Murton hit a three-run homer during a five-run first inning. Murton later added two singles, helping the Cubs' seven runs in the sixth inning and four in the ninth. In his debut with the Cubs, Juan Pierre garnered a triple and two singles. Walker contributed two doubles and a single. Also, the Cubs scored 15 runs in their 2003 season opener, defeating the Mets 15-2 at Shea Stadium.

Happy Birthday Bruce Sutter.

An All-Star in four of his five seasons with the Cubs (1976–1980) and a future Hall of Famer, Sutter was born on January 8, 1953. With a baffling split-fingered fastball, Sutter was almost unhittable in 1977, with a 1.34 ERA in 107⅓ innings. He was the first in the majors to use the pitch effectively. The ball looked like a fastball, but at the last minute, it broke like a curveball. He learned the split-fingered pitch in 1973 from Cubs minor league pitching coach Fred Martin. At the time, Sutter's career appeared to be going nowhere, but with exceptionally large hands and long fingers, he mastered the pitch to become one of the greatest relievers in baseball history. Sutter earned $75,000 in 1979 and went to arbitration over his 1980 salary. The Cubs offered $350,000 while Sutter asked for $700,000. Sutter won the case. Only eight years earlier, Hank Aaron was the highest paid player in the game at $200,000. Angered over the arbitration decision, the Cubs traded Sutter to the Cardinals at the end of the 1980 season. His plaque at Cooperstown depicts him in a Cardinals cap, although he only played for the club four seasons, compared to five with the Cubs.

On this date in 1952 . . .

Club owner P. K. Wrigley admonished general manger Wid Matthews during a bizarre press conference. At a luncheon with press, radio and television correspondents, Matthews began his annual speech about how good the Cubs were going to be next season. He said that if catcher Bruce Edwards' sore arm responded to treatment, the Cubs could build a winner around him. Mindful of the fact that the Cubs were 62-92 in 1951, their fifth consecutive losing season, Wrigley stunned the audience by interrupting and embarrassing Matthews. "I believe it's about time we stopped our daydreaming and wishful thinking and face things as they are," Wrigley said. "At the moment I will regard Edwards as no more than a patched-up ballplayer out of whom we hope to get as much service as possible until we get someone better. If and when his arm heals, there will be time to celebrate." Wrigley further stated that there was little hope for fans to expect improvement in 1952. The Cubs didn't post a winning season between 1946 and 1963.

On this date in 1963 . . .

P. K. Wrigley hired Robert Whitlow to man the newly created position of athletic director. Whitlow was a recently retired Air Force colonel who was the first athletic director at the Air Force Academy. His only baseball experience was as a college pitcher at UCLA, and he admitted that he had seen only four or five major league games during the previous five years. Whitlow had many ideas about conditioning, diet and the use of computers to spot trends and formulate strategy that later became commonplace in baseball. Whitlow's inexperience in the sport gave him no credibility, however. He was ignored by general manager John Holland and manager Bob Kennedy. He resigned in January 1965, and the club abolished the position of athletic director.

11
January

On this date in 1977 . . .

The Cubs traded Rick Monday and Mike Garman to the Dodgers for Bill Buckner, Ivan DeJesus and Jeff Albert. It proved to be an excellent deal, as Buckner and DeJesus were starters for the Cubs for several years. Buckner hit an even .300 in eight seasons in Chicago and won the NL batting title in 1980. He would probably like to forget May 24, 1982, however, when he scuffled with manager Lee Elia during an 8-2 loss to the Padres in San Diego. The two fought in the sixth inning in the runway outside the Cubs dugout. Buckner had asked pitcher Dan Larson to throw at San Diego hitters after a Tim Lollar pitch hit Buckner the prior inning. After Buckner visited the mound, Larson hit the Padres' Tim Flannery. Elia, realizing what had occurred, felt undermined and confronted Buckner. No serious blows occurred during the scuffle, although Buckner did remove himself from the game the following night, claiming his neck was injured. Elia stated publicly he did not believe the injury was serious enough to keep Buckner out of the lineup.

12
January

On this date in 1934 . . .

The Cubs announced their radio broadcasting plans for the upcoming season. The first ever Cubs game on radio took place in 1924. Hal Totten was at the mike over station WMAQ. All Cubs home games were on radio that season. In 1934, the club allowed any station to broadcast from Wrigley Field with the provision that between 10 a.m. and 3:30 p.m., each of the stations air five different times, a 25-word message advertising that day's game. Stations WGN, WCFL, WIND, WBBM and WJJD took the Cubs up on the offer. Play-by-play announcers were Bob Elson (WGN), Johnny O'Hara (WIND), Pat Flanagan (WBBM), John Harrington (WJJD) and Totten (WCFL). In addition, stations in places such as Rock Island, Illinois; Lincoln, Nebraska; and Des Moines, Iowa, did telegraphic re-creations of Cubs games. In a joint venture with the White Sox, the Cubs began charging for the right to broadcast games from Wrigley Field and Comiskey Park in 1937. WGN and WBBM each paid $7,500, while WIND, WCFL and WJJD each paid the two clubs $3,000.

13 January

The question of the day.

How many numbers have been retired by the Cubs?

The club has retired the numbers of four players who have played for the club. They first retired Ernie Banks' number 14 in 1982. Billy Williams' number 26 was retired in 1987. Recently, the club retired Ron Santo's number 10 in 2003 and Ryne Sandberg's number 23 in 2005. In addition, Major League Baseball retired number 42 in honor of Jackie Robinson in 1997. The Cubs also have not issued the number 31 in several seasons, including 2007 and 2008. Cubs' greats Greg Maddux and Ferguson Jenkins both wore the number. Retired numbers are commemorated on pinstriped flags flying from the foul poles at Wrigley Field.

14 January

On this date in 1896 . . .

A Chicago jury acquitted Cubs outfielder Walt Wilmot of charges of violating the Sabbath law by playing baseball on Sunday. The trial was the result of his arrest during the game before a packed house of 14,000 at West Side Grounds in Chicago on June 23, 1895. A pressure group called the "Sunday Observance League," led by Reverend W. W. Clark, held up play for about five minutes in the third inning when the entire Cubs team was arrested for "aiding and abetting the forming of a noisy crowd on a Sunday." Clark had been watching the contest from a rooftop on Wood Street behind the left-field fence and took the names of Cubs players. He then secured warrants from Justice Cleveland of Norwood Park. The players filed to the clubhouse in center field, and five constables served the warrants. Cubs owner James Hart posted bond, amounting to $100 per player, and the game resumed. Hart invited Clark to stay for the remainder of the game, but the reverend refused. The Cubs went on to trounce Cleveland 13-4. Charges against the other Chicago players were subsequently dropped, and the way was cleared for Sunday baseball in the Windy City in the future.

On this date in 1942 . . .

President Franklin Roosevelt gave baseball Commissioner Kenesaw Landis the go-ahead to play ball for the duration of World War II. In his statement, Roosevelt said that he believed the continuation of the sport would be beneficial to the country's morale. The war altered the sport over the next four seasons, as most of those eligible for the Armed Forces were drafted or enlisted. During the war, a number of benefit games were played with the entire gate receipts earmarked for wartime charities. All major league games on June 6, 1944, were postponed in observance of the D-Day landing in France. On August 1, 1945, five days before the dropping of the atom bomb on Hiroshima, Japan, a total of 4,044 women were admitted free to Wrigley Field for a game against the Pirates by bringing cakes and cookies for the Chicago Servicemen's Center. The Cubs closed the 1945 season by winning the National League pennant, but lost the World Series to the Detroit Tigers in seven games.

On this date in 1916 . . .

Chewing gum magnate William Wrigley, Jr. became a minority stockholder in the Cubs, purchasing a share for $50,000. Born in Philadelphia in 1861, Wrigley started in the family soap business. He gave away sticks of gum to housewives as an inducement to buy his wares. Wrigley found the gum to be so popular that he embarked on a business of manufacturing it in 1910 and made a fortune. Once he bought a piece of the Cubs, Wrigley became a passionate baseball fan and bought larger and larger shares of the franchise. By 1919, he had controlling interest in the club. William died in 1932, and the Cubs passed to his son Philip Knight (P. K.) Wrigley. P. K. retained control of the club until his death in 1977. The Wrigley family sold the Cubs to the Tribune Company on June 16, 1991 for $20.5 million.

17
January

Happy Birthday Hank Leiber.

Hank Leiber, an outfielder with the Cubs from 1939 through 1941, was born on January 17, 1911. Known for his plate-crowding batting stance, Leiber played his last major league game at age 31 because of three major head injuries. The last one occurred on June 23, 1941, when a fastball hurled by Giants pitcher Cliff Melton during a 1-0 Chicago win beaned Leiber in the head. Ironically, the injury came three days after the Cubs received a shipment of one-ounce plastic shields that could be inserted into a player's regulation cap to help protect him if hit in the head by a pitch. Leiber refused to wear one, however. Major league clubs first used the shields during the 1941 season. Batting helmets did not become commonplace until the 1950s.

18
January

The question of the day.

Who is the only pitcher to win 200 games while playing for the Cubs?

Charlie Root is the only pitcher to win at least 200 games in a Cub uniform. Perhaps best known for throwing Babe Ruth's famous "called shot" during the 1932 World Series, Root was 201-156 as a Cub from 1926 through 1941, winning game number 200 at the age of 42. He's also first in games pitched (605) and innings pitched (3,137⅓). He was at the center of a publicity stunt during a Cubs game against the Reds on September 4, 1938. Root pitched to pilot Douglas Corrigan, who had become an overnight celebrity seven weeks earlier on July 17. Federal aviation authorities refused to allow Corrigan to fly his rickety plane to Ireland, so he filed a flight plan from New York to California, then flew across the Atlantic Ocean to Dublin, claiming he got lost due to a faulty compass. Dubbed "Wrong Way" Corrigan, he received a hero's welcome in the United States and was honored with ticker-tape parades, receptions, banquets and a movie contract. Corrigan arrived at Crosley Field in the middle of the game, and after a short speech, grabbed a bat to face Root. On Root's second pitch, Corrigan tapped the ball back to the mound and ran to third base to the delight of the crowd.

The question of the day.

Where did the Cubs play their first regular-season game in 2000?

The Cubs opened the 2000 campaign in Tokyo against the Mets, and won 5-3 before 55,000 at the Tokyo Dome. It was the first regular-season game ever played outside of North America and the earliest date for a Cubs opener in club history. The contest began at 7:06 p.m. Tokyo time, which was 4:06 a.m. in Chicago. Shane Andrews and Mark Grace both went deep in Don Baylor's debut as Chicago's manager. Sammy Sosa delivered a single, a double and walked twice. After the game was over, he met with Crown Prince Naruhito and Princess Masako. Jon Lieber was the winning pitcher. The two teams met again the following day, and the Mets won 5-1 in 11 innings. Benny Agbayani drove in the winning runs with a pinch-hit grand slam off Danny Young. It was Young's major league debut.

The Inauguration Day question.

How many sitting U.S. Presidents have watched the Cubs play in person?

There have been five who have witnessed a total of seven games.
The following is a list of those Chief Executives:

President	Date and Opponent	Result	Location
William Howard Taft	5-29-1909 vs. Pirates	W, 8-3	Pittsburgh
William Howard Taft	9-16-1909 vs. Giants	L, 1-2	Chicago
William Howard Taft	5-2-1910 vs. Pirates	L, 2-5	Pittsburgh
Herbert Hoover*	10-14-1929 vs. Athletics	L, 2-3	Philadelphia
Ronald Reagan	9-30-1988 vs. Pirates	L, 9-10	Chicago
Bill Clinton	6-30-1999 vs. Brewers	W, 5-4	Chicago
George W. Bush	4-3-2006 vs. Reds	W, 16-7	Cincinnati

*World Series

In addition, First Lady Hillary Clinton attended a game at Wrigley Field on April 4, 1994. Charles P. Taft, the half brother of William Howard Taft, owned stock in the Cubs from 1905 through 1915.

The question of the day.

What is the smallest crowd in the history of Wrigley Field?

The Cubs drew a "crowd" of 314 to a 7-4 win over the Phillies on September 24, 1943. With sellouts at Wrigley Field the norm, it is difficult to believe there was a time in which crowds numbered in the hundreds. Game-by-game attendance records are available from the 1938 season to the present. The smallest crowds at Wrigley during that time frame were usually at the end of a losing season during a late-September cold snap and are contained in the following list:

Date	Attendance	Date	Attendance
September 24, 1943	314	September 24, 1962	629
September 21, 1966	530	September 26, 1962	930
September 16, 1965	550	September 19, 1965	892
September 28, 1962	595	September 14, 1966	961
September 17, 1959	598	September 22, 1966	961
September 27, 1962	617		

The question of the day.

Why do the outfield walls at Wrigley Field curve away from home plate near the foul lines?

The present day bleachers at Wrigley Field were built during the 1937 season and 1937–1938 off-season. Originally, the bleachers were supposed to hold 5,000 fans, with the foul lines about 20 to 25 feet closer than they are today. There were numerous complaints that this would be too much of a home run target, however, and the size of the bleachers was reduced to 3,000 by creating the curving "cutaways" down the foul lines that are still one of the many unique features at Wrigley Field. Renovations during the 2005–2006 off-season expanded the bleachers by 1,900 seats. The foul lines at the ballpark are the longest in major league baseball. It is 355 feet down the left-field line and 353 feet to the right. The next longest foul lines are at Coors Field in Denver, which are 347 feet to the left-field fence and 350 to the right.

The question of the day.

How much of Wrigley Field is in the same location as it was when the ballpark opened in 1914?

The only part of Wrigley Field still standing in the same spot as in 1914, are 11 sections roughly from a point behind first base to the end of the stands at Sheffield Avenue. The location of the starting point of the original stands is still visible today with the "dogleg" at the first base dugout. During the 1922–1923 off-season, the ballpark, then known as Cubs Park, was expanded. The grandstand was cut into three parts. The right-field and left-field wings were separated from the section behind home plate. Eleven sections of the right-field wing were retained in their original positions. The left-field wing was placed on rollers and moved 60 feet north toward Waveland Avenue. The Cubs purchased a nearby property that was more than 100 feet in width that gave them the space to expand the size of the ballpark. The space allowed them to move the center section of the stands toward the Clark and Addison corner. Wrigley added the upper decks in 1927 and 1928, and the name of the ballpark changed from Cubs Park to Wrigley Field. The present day bleachers were constructed in 1937 and 1938.

Happy Birthday Jack Brickhouse.

Legendary Chicago broadcaster Jack Brickhouse was born on this date in 1916. He was the Cubs announcer on radio and television from 1940 until his retirement in 1981. WGN radio hired Brickhouse in 1940 to broadcast both the Cubs and White Sox games as a duo with Bob Elson. When WGN television went on the air in 1948, Brickhouse still did the games for both Chicago teams. From 1948 through 1967, the Cubs and Sox had an agreement in which only home games would be telecast. The Sox ended the pact in 1968, and the two franchises had their own exclusive broadcasting teams. Brickhouse went to the Cubs while Elson became the White Sox's main announcer. Brickhouse was also the play-by-play announcer for the Chicago Bears and Chicago Bulls. The team honored him at Wrigley Field on August 5, 1979, on the occasion of his 5,000th broadcast. Brickhouse received a plaque with the names of almost 800 Cubs, a stained glass replica of Wrigley Field and a "sofa" made out of the bats of famous players. He died in 1998. A year later, the Cubs organization placed Brickhouse's trademark phrase "Hey, Hey" above the distance markers on both foul pole screens.

25 January

On this date in 1899 . . .

The Cubs traded Bill Dahlen to the Dodgers for Gene DeMontreville. Dahlen played shortstop for the Cubs from 1891 through 1898 and was in the majors from 1891 through 1911. He is arguably the best 19th century player that is not in the Hall of Fame. Dahlen still holds the all-time Cubs record for the longest hitting streak in club history at 42 games in 1894. The streak ended in unusual fashion on August 7. Much of West Side Grounds in Chicago was in ruins from a devastating fire two days earlier. The burnt area was fenced off, and fans sat on the left side of the diamond. The Cubs won 13-11 over the Reds, but Dahlen was hitless in six at-bats. Strangely, the hitters surrounding him had big days. Jimmy Ryan, batting lead off just ahead of Dahlen, collected five hits, and Walt Wilmot, batting third behind Dahlen, also had five hits. The day after Dahlen's 42-game streak ended, he started another one that lasted 28 games, giving him hits in 70 of 71 games. The 28-game streak is the third longest in Cubs history, tied with a similar streak by Ron Santo in 1966. The second longest is a 30-game streak by Jerome Walton in 1989.

26 January

On this date in 1932 . . .

P. K. Wrigley took over as owner of the Cubs at age 37 following the death of his father. Despite his very public position as head of both the Cubs and the Wrigley Gum Company, Wrigley had a passion for anonymity. P. K. rarely attended games at Wrigley Field, preferring to follow the club on radio and later on television. When he did attend games, it was usually incognito, in which he took a seat among ordinary fans in the upper deck. His 45-year reign as head of the club was marked by some early success, and the club won four NL pennants from 1932 through 1945. But that was followed by one losing season after another, and Wrigley's devotion to baseball and competence as an owner came into question. Like many casual fans, Wrigley had some silly notions about what it took to build a winning team, but unlike most casual fans, he had the authority to implement his ideas. To make matters worse, Wrigley was often difficult and liked to be different just for the sake of being different. His most controversial decision was a refusal to install lights for night games. On the positive side, he improved Wrigley Field and transformed it into the most beautiful sports edifice in America.

On this date in 1992 . . .

The Cubs traded Ivan DeJesus to the Phillies for Larry Bowa and Ryne Sandberg. The Sandberg trade is the best in Cubs history and is considered one of the greatest in baseball history. Sandberg was considered just a throw in, initially. It was seen as essentially a swap of starting shortstops, and Sandberg was added to even up the deal. At first, the Cubs did not know where to play him. "The kid is capable of playing a couple of positions," said general manager Dallas Green of Sandberg. "He can play shortstop, second base or the outfield." In the Phillies minor league system, Sandberg was a shortstop. Philadelphia included him in the deal because the club believed that both Julio Franco and Juan Samuel were better prospects. Prior to his arrival in Chicago, Sandberg had played in just 13 big-league games, mainly as a defensive replacement at shortstop and as a pinch runner. He had one hit in six at-bats. At the beginning of the 1982 season, Sandberg was the Cubs' starting third baseman. He moved to second base in September of that season, supplanting Bump Wills and making his mark as one of the best second basemen in the game.

The question of the day.

Why are Chinese elm trees a part of Wrigley Field lore?

When the bleachers were constructed in 1937 and 1938, club owner P. K. Wrigley ordered the construction of large platforms leading to the scoreboard. To compliment the ivy, they placed Chinese elms on the platforms as a decorative touch. However, the trees could not survive the strong winds and harsh Chicago winters. After several attempts and about two dozen dead trees, Wrigley gave up on the idea. The empty platforms remained a unique feature of the ballpark at the back of the bleachers.

The question of the day.

How did World War II help the Cubs win the 1945 pennant?

By the start of the 1945 season, the United States had been involved militarily in World War II for three years and five months. By that time, nearly every able-bodied man between the ages of 18 and 40 were in the service. The wartime pennant of 1945 was possible because the Cubs were able to put together a semblance of a major league team with players such as Stan Hack, Phil Cavarretta, Andy Pafko, Bill Nicholson, Peanuts Lowrey, Claude Passeau, Hank Wyse, Paul Derringer and Hank Borowy due to medical military deferments issued to those players. The best Cubs players who were in the military during the 1945 season were Clyde McCullough, Johnny Schmitz, Eddie Waitkus and Marv Rickert. The Cardinals came into the 1945 campaign as the odds-on favorites because they had won the pennant in 1942, 1943 and 1944 by wide margins. St. Louis was without such stars as Stan Musial, Enos Slaughter, Walker Cooper and Howie Pollet in 1945, yet finished only three games behind the Cubs. If both the Cubs and the Cardinals had been at full strength, Chicago likely would not have come close to finishing in first place.

The question of the day.

What is the "Billy Goat Curse"?

Some blame the failure of the Cubs to reach the World Series since 1945 on the "Billy Goat Curse" placed on the club by restaurant owner Billy Sianis, whose goat, Sonovia, was the restaurant's mascot. Sianis bought two tickets to the fourth game of the 1945 World Series: one for him and for Sonovia. Sianis was denied admission to Wrigley Field unless he left the goat outside. A bitter Sianis put a hex on the Cubs and said they would never play in the World Series again, implementing the now-infamous "Billy Goat Curse." The Cubs went on to lose the Series against the Tigers in seven games. Sianis died during the 1970s without seeing another World Series in Wrigley Field, and as most good Cubs fans know, there has yet to be one to this day. At the Wrigley Field opener in 1982, the Cubs invited Sam Sianis, Billy's nephew, and his goat onto the playing field to lift the curse. The Cubs also brought back Sam and his goat in 1994 after the Cubs lost 12 home games in a row. Saturday Night Live brought national recognition to the Billy Goat Tavern in a recurring skit about the restaurant that featured Chicago natives John Belushi and Bill Murray hollering "Cheeseburger! Cheeseburger! Cheeseburger! No Pepsi! Coke! No Fries! Chips!"

31 January

On this date in 1947 . . .

Johnny Kling died. Kling was a standout catcher for the Cubs from 1900 through 1911. His best years were in 1906, 1907 and 1908, when the Cubs played in the World Series three consecutive seasons and won the world title in 1907 and 1908. Kling decided to hold out the entire 1909 season, however, in a salary dispute. He spent part of the year as the player-manager of a semi-pro team in his hometown of Kansas City, Missouri. He also operated a large two-story billiards parlor and found time to win the 1909 world pocket billiards championship. In his absence, the Cubs posted a record of 104-49, but finished second to the Pirates, who were 110-42. Kling returned to the Cubs in 1910, and the club reached the World Series again. On April 25 of that year, Kling appeared on the stage of a Chicago music hall demonstrating his skill with a pool cue by playing a match against Cubs legend Cap Anson. After his playing days ended, Kling became a successful real estate developer and owned the minor league Kansas City Blues from 1933 through 1937.

Wrigley Hits 100

February

01
February

On this date in 1898 . . .

The Cubs released Cap Anson as both a player and a manager. Anson had been a player with the Cubs since 1876 and a player-manager since 1879. He played on six National League championship teams and managed five, although the last one was in 1886. Anson was let go following a ninth place finish (in a 12-team league) and a 59-73 record in 1897, with a team Anson claimed was full of "drunkards and loafers." Although never on good terms with Jim Hart, who took over as club president in 1891, the two grew increasingly antagonistic toward each other throughout the years. Hart regarded Anson as a relic of the past who was unwilling to change with the times, while Anson saw Hart as a meddler who undermined his authority and refused to pay the salaries needed to build a winning team. Nonetheless, it was a shock for fans to see a Chicago team without Anson at the helm after 22 years with the club. Because of his absence, newspapers began referring to the club as the "Orphans," a nickname that persisted for several seasons.

02
February

On this date in 1876 . . .

The National League was officially organized during meetings at the Grand Central Hotel in New York City. The eight-team league included teams from Boston, Chicago, Cincinnati, Hartford, Louisville, New York, Philadelphia and St. Louis. William Hulbert, a wealthy grain and coal merchant, was instrumental in organizing the league and became the president of the Chicago club, first-called the White Stockings. The new National League required each team to play 70 games, which usually meant playing three times per week. The games were generally played on Tuesdays, Thursdays and Saturdays, and admission was 50 cents. Sunday games were prohibited, as well as the sale of liquor. The coveted prize to the season champions of this new league was a pennant worth $100. Of the eight original clubs, only the Chicago and Boston franchises have operated continuously since 1876. Chicago is the only one to have operated in one city since the birth of the league. The Boston club moved to Milwaukee in 1953 and Atlanta in 1966. In 2008, the Cubs became the first franchise in sports history to win 10,000 games in one city.

The question of the day.

Who is Emil Verban?

Emil Verban was a Cubs infielder from 1948 through 1950. He hit a respectable .280 in 629 at-bats, but only managed one home run. In 1975, six individuals in Washington formed the Emil Verban Memorial Society as a Cubs fan club because they saw Verban as the epitome of a good Cubs player, a hard working, solid contributor who flew relatively under the radar. Lobbyist Bruce Ladd headed the group, and one of the six original members was Dick Cheney, then White House Chief of Staff under Gerald Ford. The word "memorial" was added, even though Verban was alive and well (he lived until 1989). "I picked Emil because he was so obscure," said Ladd. "We had all seen him play and could relate to him." At first, Verban thought they were mocking him and was insulted by the use of his name. However, the negative feelings later dissipated when society member President Ronald Reagan honored him with a trip to the White House. Other prominent members include former First Lady Hillary Clinton, Justice Harry Blackmun of the United States Supreme Court, television broadcaster Bryant Gumbel, actor Tom Bosley and columnists David Broder and George Will.

On this date in 1909 . . .

John Clarkson, a pitcher for the Cubs from 1884 through 1887, died. Pitchers during the 1880s were expected to take the mound at least three times per week, which allowed him to set club records that will never be broken. In 1885, he started 70 games and finished on the mound in an amazing 68 of them. Clarkson pitched 623 innings and had a won-lost record of 53-16. Ten of his victories were shutouts, including one no-hitter. Although Clarkson was one of the best pitchers in the game, club owner Albert Spalding and manager Cap Anson grew tired of his temperamental ways. Clarkson would often sulk when criticized or when things did not go his way. He was sold to Boston on April 3, 1888, for $10,000, a choice the club would come to regret. After leaving Chicago, Clarkson had a won-lost record of 192-120 and finished his career with 328 wins. He spent most of the last three years of his life in a mental institution in Massachusetts and died of pneumonia at age 47. Clarkson was elected to the Baseball Hall of Fame in 1963.

05 February

Happy Birthday Max Flack.

Max Flack was born on this day in 1890. On May 30, 1922, the Cubs traded him to the Cardinals for Cliff Heathcote between games of a morning-afternoon double-header in Chicago. Flack and Heathcote both appeared in the morning game, won 4-1 by the Cubs. They then traded uniforms and played for their new clubs in the afternoon game, a 3-1 Chicago victory. Heathcote was 0-for-3 as a Cardinal and 2-for-4 as a Cub. Flack went 0-for-4 in the first game and 1-for-4 in the second. Ironically, the two men overall had remarkably similar careers. Flack played in 1,411 games and Heathcote in 1,415. Heathcote hit .275 for his career, which was not too far behind Flack's .278 lifetime batting average. Both men scared pitchers with their big leads and quick feet, combining for 390 stolen bases, with Flack's number just edging Heathcote's at 200 total stolen. Heathcote, however, held the advantage in home runs with 42 to Flack's 35. For 62 years, the two maintained the status of the only players in major league history to play for two teams in one day until Joel Youngblood played for both the Mets and the Expos on August 4, 1982.

06 February

Happy Birthday Ronald Reagan.

Reagan was born on this date in 1911 in Tampico, Illinois. During the 1930s, Reagan did telegraphic re-creations of Cubs and White Sox games from radio station WHO in Des Moines, Iowa. The play-by-play accounts were sent via telegraph from Wrigley Field and Comiskey Park to the station, and Reagan would relay the information to listeners. In 1936, the Sporting News conducted a reader poll to determine the most popular radio play-by-play broadcaster in the country. Despite being on air in the relatively small city of Des Moines and never calling a live game, Reagan finished ninth in the poll. He fared much better in future elections, winning two terms as both the Governor of California and the President of the United States. While residing in the White House, Reagan visited Wrigley Field on September 30, 1988, where he threw out the first pitch and did an inning of play-by-play with Harry Caray. The game went to 10 innings and ended in a 10-9 loss to the Pirates.

Happy Birthday Burt Hooton.

Burt Hooton was born on this date in 1950. On April 16, 1972, almost two months after his 22nd birthday, and in only his fourth career start, he pitched a no-hitter, defeating the Phillies 4-0 on a cold, rainy day before 9,583 fans at Wrigley Field. Hooton threw 118 pitches, walked seven and struck out seven. A howling wind not only helped preserve the no-hitter, but the shutout as well, keeping a seventh inning drive by Greg Luzinski just inside the wall where outfielder Rick Monday could make the play. In the ninth inning, Willie Montanez grounded to Glenn Beckert at second base, Deron Johnson struck out on a 3-2 pitch and Luzinski fanned with the count 0-2 to end the game. With the help of his unique knuckle-curve, Hooton pitched 30 innings in his first four starts and allowed only five earned runs and eight hits. It looked as though the Cubs had found a number two starter to team with Ferguson Jenkins, but it never happened. Hooton struggled after his no-hitter and was traded to the Dodgers in 1975 with a record of 34-44 as a Cub. He blossomed in Los Angeles and was 96-63 as a Dodger from 1975 through 1981, pitching in three World Series. In exchange for Hooton, the Cubs received Geoff Zahn and Eddie Solomon, two hurlers who never won a game in a Chicago uniform.

The question of the day.

When did the logo with the smaller letters "UBS" appearing inside the larger letter "C" first show up on a Cubs uniform?

The logo first appeared in 1909 when the Cubs added an embellishment to the uniforms with the letters "UBS" inside a circular "C." That season, it was used only on the road uniforms. The home jerseys had a brown bear holding a bat inside the letter "C." The "UBS" letters inside the "C" were used on the road uniforms again in 1910, disappeared for nine seasons and returned in 1919. The emblem was used on-and-off for two decades before becoming a permanent part of the uniform. It has been used on the home shirts every season since 1937.

09 February

Happy Birthday Heinie Zimmerman.

Heinie Zimmerman, a Cub from 1907 through 1916, was born on this date in 1887. Zimmerman's notorious temper caused frequent conflicts with umpires, which led to numerous ejections from games. On June 19, 1913, a concerned fan with a sense of humor, in an attempt to curtail Zimmerman's untimely outbursts, gave Zimmerman half of a $100 bill, with Harvey Woodruff, a sports editor with the Chicago Tribune, serving as intermediary. Woodruff told Zimmerman that if he did not get thrown out of a game for the next two weeks, the fan would send the other half of the bill. On July 2, the last day of the two-week probationary period, in a game against the Pirates in Chicago, Zimmerman attempted to steal home and umpire Ernie Quigley called him tagged out at the plate. Zimmerman jumped to his feet to begin arguing with Quigley but suddenly seemed to remember the bribe, calming down quickly and walking away quietly. Surprisingly, he did complete his end of the bargain and received the other half of the $100 bill before the next game.

10 February

On this date in 1914 . . .

Cubs owner Charles Murphy announced that player-manager Johnny Evers had resigned. Evers hit the roof when he heard the news and denied that he resigned. Evers claimed Murphy had fired him because of disagreements over his managerial style and temperament. Murphy believed that Evers made decisions based largely on emotion, instead of with reason. Evers' demand of an increase in salary also led to his dismissal. Before the 1913 season, he signed a contract calling for $10,000 per year over four seasons. Charles Weeghman, owner of the Chicago Federal League team, offered Evers a $30,000 bonus and a five-year, $75,000 contract to jump. Evers gave the Cubs an opportunity to match the offer, but Murphy refused and released Evers. The National League, fighting to keep as many stars as possible in the wake of the threat from the Federal League, would not honor the release and instead, negotiated Evers' trade to the Boston Braves. Evers helped the Braves win the National League pennant and World Series that season, with the Cubs finishing a distant fourth.

Happy Birthday Jimmy Ryan.

A Cub from 1885 through 1900, Ryan was born on this date in 1863. He is one of the many overlooked 19th century stars who deserves a place in the Hall of Fame. Ryan is the all-time Cubs record holder for career triples, with 142. He also ranks 11th in games-played (1,660), ninth in at-bats (6,757), second in runs (1,409), eighth in hits (2,073), eighth in doubles (362) and ninth in RBIs (914). Ryan also pitched on occasion and had a record of 6-1 with two saves. On July 28, 1888, he not only hit for the cycle in a 21-17 win over Detroit in Chicago but also pitched eight innings of relief. Like many players of his era, Ryan also was handy with his fists. He punched out two different sportswriters in 1887 and 1892, and he assaulted a train conductor in 1896. This was after sustaining serious injuries when a train carrying the Cubs derailed on August 6, 1893. Ryan was cut badly on the face, head and neck and had to have a piece of glass removed from his leg. He missed the rest of the season because of the accident. In 1905, Ryan advised against the sport as a career because few players lasted long enough to make any money. "Baseball is not a permanent profession," Ryan said. "Look in the newspapers and you see that a baseball player 35 years of age is considered an old man."

12 February

On this date in 1942 . . .

The Cubs dropped plans to play night games at Comiskey Park during the upcoming season. The club had entered into discussions with the White Sox to play home games under the lights on the South Side. "We have agreed that in the best interest of the game it would be better to preserve the intense rivalries between the fans of the North and South Sides of Chicago," Cubs general manager James Gallagher said. In 1944, the Cubs applied to the recreation section of the War Production Board to install lights at Wrigley Field, but the application was denied. The board invited the Cubs to resubmit their request once the war ended, but by that time Cubs owner P. K. Wrigley had a change of heart. By 1948, the Cubs were the only team in the majors not playing a portion of the home schedule at night, a distinction the franchise would hold until 1988.

13 February

On this date in 1964 . . .

Cubs second baseman Ken Hubbs died at age 22 in a plane crash near Provo, Utah, along with lifelong friend Dennis Doyle. The ever-hustling Hubbs became a fan favorite in 1962 when he won the NL Rookie of the Year Award. Hubbs was fascinated with aviation, and during road trips, he often sat in the cockpit with the pilot. He purchased a Cessna 172 in November 1963 and began taking flying lessons. He obtained his pilot's license two weeks before the crash. He took Doyle to Provo from the pair's hometown of Colton, California, to see Doyle's wife, who was visiting her parents. On the return trip, Hubbs took off in a snowstorm. The single engine plane spiraled out of control and crashed into ice-encrusted Utah Lake, five miles from the Provo Airport. Hubbs likely lost sight of the horizon in the storm.

14 February

The question of the day.

Who was Frank "Wildfire" Schulte?

Schulte was a star outfielder for the Cubs from 1904 through 1916. He appeared in 1,564 games for the club and played in four World Series. When the cork-center baseball was introduced in 1910, Schulte was among the first to take advantage. Most hitters of the period choked up on bats with thick handles, concentrating on making contact and hitting singles. Schulte used bats with thin handles and placed his hands at the knob to generate more power. In 1911, he collected 30 doubles, 21 triples and 21 home runs, impressive figures during the Dead Ball Era. One of his drives cleared the 61-foot-high right-field wall at West Side Grounds. Schulte acquired his nickname, "Wildfire," because of his admiration for famed actress Lillian Russell. In 1908, the Cubs conducted spring training in Vicksburg, Mississippi, at the same time Russell was in town performing her play, Wildfire. She gave a party for the Cubs, and in appreciation, Schulte, who owned racehorses, named one of his trotters Wildfire. Before long, he too was known by the name. A man of many superstitions, Schulte believed that finding a hatpin guaranteed him a base hit. If either prong of the lucky pin was bent, he believed the ball would go in that direction.

15
February

The question of the day.

What was the City Series?

A largely forgotten aspect of the histories of the Cubs and the White Sox is the Chicago City Series, which was played nearly every fall from 1903 through 1942. The series was held just after the close of the regular season, at the same time as the World Series, and was a highly anticipated event in Chicago. Weekend games usually drew capacity crowds, and those played on weekday afternoons drew well above the regular-season figures, even though they were held in the city's fickle October weather. Attendance remained high even in seasons that both clubs finished with losing records. From 1903 through 1942, the Cubs and the White Sox met in the postseason 26 times, with the White Sox winning 19 times, the Cubs six and one draw in 1903. In 1906, both the Cubs and the White Sox won their league championships and met in the World Series, with the Sox taking the title four games to two. Although fan interest was still high, the clubs played their last City Series in 1942. Cubs management, led by P. K. Wrigley and Charlie Grimm, had not won a City Series since 1930, were embarrassed by the one-sided nature of the affair and declined to play in any more of them. Wrigley stated that it was a "booby prize" unworthy of the effort.

16
February

Happy Birthday Jerry Hairston, Jr.

Jerry Hairston, Jr. played for the Cubs in 2005 and 2006. He is part of the only three-generation African-American family in major league history and one of just three families overall with three generations to have played in the big leagues. His grandfather Sammy was a long-time Negro League star who played four games with the White Sox in 1951. Sammy had two sons in the big leagues. Jerry, Sr. played in 859 games, 808 of them with the White Sox, from 1973 through 1989. Johnny Hairston appeared in three contests with the Cubs in 1969. Jerry Sr. has two sons in the majors, both active in 2008. Jerry, Jr. made his debut in 1998 with the Orioles and played for the Reds in 2008. Scott Hairston played his first game with the Diamondbacks in 2004 and was a member of the Padres in 2008. The Bells were the first three-generation family in the majors. Grandfather Gus played from 1950 through 1964, followed by his son Buddy (1972–1989) and Buddy's sons David (1995–2006) and Mike (2000). The other three-generation family is the Boones, consisting of Ray (1948–1960), his son Bob (1972–1990) and Bob's sons Bret (1992–2005) and Aaron, who debuted in 1997 and was still active in 2008.

17
February

On this date in 1887 . . .

The Cubs sold future Hall of Famer King Kelly to Boston for a then-record price of $10,000. Team owner Albert Spalding and manager Cap Anson were angry over the loss to the St. Louis Browns during the 1886 World Series and grew tired of the drinking escapades, insubordination and high salary demands of many of the players. Additionally during the off-season, the Cubs sold Kelly's outfield mates to other clubs. They shipped George Gore to the Giants and Abner Dalrymple to Pittsburgh. Pitcher Jim McCormick also went to Pittsburgh. The sale of the players, especially the enormously popular Kelly, enraged the Chicago faithful. Cubs' fans harassed Anson throughout the 1887 season, and many at West Side Park openly rooted for the opposition. On June 24, when Kelly played his first game in Chicago wearing a Boston uniform, fans presented him with flowers. The Cubs slipped from first place with a 90-34 record in 1886, to 71-50 and third place in 1887. The Cubs did not win another National League pennant until 1906.

18
February

On this date in 1950 . . .

The Cubs hired Wid Matthews as general manager. Matthews lasted nearly seven years on the job and was an unmitigated disaster. During that period, the club did not have a winning season, with records of 64-89, 62-92, 77-77, 65-89, 64-90, 72-81 and 60-94. He came to the Cubs after working in the Dodgers' front office under Branch Rickey, who had built dynasties in both St. Louis and Brooklyn. Matthews possessed unbridled enthusiasm, and at the end of each season he stated that the Cubs were only a player or two away from a pennant and boldly predicted that success was just around the corner. He announced a "five-year plan" that would bring the Cubs back to contention. Wid's approach was less than scientific. When asked how he sized up a prospect, Matthews said, "When I shake hands with a boy and he has a good grip, that's one of the essentials. Then I pat him on the shoulder to see how muscular he is." Matthews apparently learned little from Rickey on how to build a pennant-winning team and was fired at the end of the 1956 season.

On this date in 1987 . . .

Harry Caray suffered a stroke while playing cards at a country club near his winter home in Palm Springs, California. Caray missed the first six weeks of the regular season during his recovery. In the meantime, the Cubs used celebrity announcers on a one-game basis. Brent Musburger did the play-by-play on Opening Day, and his successors included Bill Murray, George Wendt, Jim Belushi, Dan Aykroyd, Bob Costas, Ernie Harwell, Dick Enberg, Pat Summerall, Bryant Gumbel, Gary Bender, Jack Buck, Ernie Banks, Mike Royko, George Will and Stan Musial. When he returned to the booth on May 19, Caray received a congratulatory phone call from President Ronald Reagan. "You've had a lot of celebrities fill in during your recovery," Reagan said, "but there's nothing like the real thing."

On this date in 1943 . . .

P. K. Wrigley announced the formation of the All-American Girls Professional Baseball League. Wrigley thought that World War II would decimate the major league's playing talent and believed a women's league would be a way to keep the ballparks busy and the fans entertained. Teams formed in Rockford, Illinois; South Bend, Indiana; Racine, Wisconsin; and Kenosha, Wisconsin. In 1943 and 1944, the league staged games at Wrigley Field under temporary lights, the first night baseball games ever played at Clark and Addison. The league had tremendous success and reached its peak in 1948, when ten teams attracted nearly a million spectators. Despite its popularity, the league remained a regional attraction, never expanding beyond the borders of Illinois, Wisconsin, Indiana and Michigan. Although the women played hard-nosed ball, an emphasis was placed on femininity. Beauty consultant Helena Rubinstein was brought in to talk about make-up, how to walk, how to take off a coat and how to deal with male fans. Short hair and slacks were prohibited. The uniforms were short skirts designed to show as much leg as possible. The league dissolved in 1954, but interest was revived with the 1992 film *A League of Their Own*.

21
February

Happy Birthday Adam Greenberg.

Adam Greenberg was born on this date in 1981. He made his major league debut with the Cubs on July 9, 2005, pinch-hitting in the eighth inning of an 8-2 win over the Marlins in Miami. In what can only be described as a terrible twist of fate, the first pitch of his first major league at bat, a 91mile-per-hour fastball thrown by Valerio de los Santos, struck Greenberg in the head. He was placed on the disabled list with a severe concussion and suffered excruciating headaches for months, bringing his brief major league experience to a screeching halt. Through 2008, Greenberg had yet to appear in another big-league game. That season, he played at the Class AA level in the Angels organization.

22
February

On this date in 1946 . . .

Training camp opened on Catalina Island, off the coast of Los Angeles. It was the first training camp held in peacetime in five years. The 1946 training camps were unique, as returning World War II veterans competed with wartime fill-ins for spots on the roster. The Cubs spring training camp included 20 players who spent the entire 1945 season in the military. Some, like Johnny Schmitz, Eddie Waitkus, Clyde McCullough, Paul Erickson, Marv Rickert and Emil Kush, were regulars with the Cubs in 1946, others were not so lucky. Catalina Island was the spring training home of the Cubs from 1921 through 1942 and again from 1946 through 1951. It is 22 miles long and eight miles wide and located 22 miles south-southwest of Los Angeles. William Wrigley, Jr. bought controlling interest in the company that operated the island in 1919 and began to develop it as a tourist attraction. In 1975, P. K. Wrigley, William's son, deeded the family shares to the Catalina Island Conservancy, which now stewards 88 percent of the island.

On this date in 1979 . . .

The Cubs traded Manny Trillo, Dave Rader and Greg Gross to the Phillies for Barry Foote, Jerry Martin, Ted Sizemore, Derek Botelho and Henry Mack. Sizemore would not last long in Chicago. The August 2, 1979, game against the Expos in Montreal did not end until 2:40 a.m. on August 3 because of three rain delays. This upset the Cubs' travel plans because planes could not fly out of the Canadian city between midnight and 6 a.m., and the club was scheduled to play the Cardinals in Chicago that afternoon. To help soothe frayed nerves after a 6-4 loss, the club's sixth in a row, and the difficult travel itinerary, Cubs management treated the players to a dinner at a posh restaurant. Management placed a two-bottle limit of wine per table (at $40 per bottle), but Sizemore and Dick Tidrow angrily walked out because of the restriction placed on their alcohol consumption. Sizemore continued to complain loudly on both the bus ride to the airport and on the flight to Chicago. Two weeks later, they traded him to the Red Sox.

The question of the day.

Who were the Grubby Cubbies?

In August 1978, with the club three games out of first place, many of the Cubs players grew beards to make themselves look more fierce on the field and to give the team a new identity. Bruce Sutter hatched the idea that earned his team the nickname "Grubby Cubbies." General manager Bob Kennedy, who was a Marine fighter pilot during both World War II and the Korean War, was less-than-thrilled with the fashion statement. "If they want to look like idiots that's all right with me," Kennedy said. Manager Herman Franks took a different approach. "If it helps them win, let 'em grow 'em down to the ground," Franks said. "I'll try and grow one myself if we're in first place in September." Unfortunately, the beards did not help, and the Cubs finished in third place, 11 games behind the first place Phillies. Sutter kept his beard for the rest of his career, however. He is depicted with a beard on his Hall of Fame plaque in Cooperstown.

Happy Birthday Ron Santo.

Ron Santo was born on this date in 1940. He has long-deserved admission to the Hall of Fame, but so far, has been unable to gain the necessary votes. First, the Baseball Writers' Association of America denied his entry, as did the Veterans Committee in as recently as 2007. Santo played for the Cubs from 1960 through 1973, was named to five All-Star teams and won five Gold Gloves. He has been in the broadcast booth since 1990. Santo's accomplishments are all the more remarkable because he has done so while battling diabetes. He was diagnosed with the disease in 1958, but kept it a secret until 1971. He made the disclosure at the urging of the Diabetes Association of Chicago. The hope was to prove that diabetes could lead to an ordinary life, or in the case of Santo, an extraordinary life. He took an insulin shot every day while playing and kept candy bars on the bench in case he experienced a low blood sugar. During an 11-year span from 1961 through 1971, Santo missed only 31 games. Santo's struggle with diabetes continues today. Doctors amputated his right leg below the knee in 2001, as a complication of the disease. In 2002, his left leg also was amputated.

On this date in 2004 . . .

The "Steve Bartman ball" was destroyed. Bartman interfered with a playable fly ball sailing down Wrigley's left-field wall in game six of the 2003 National League Championship Series with the Cubs just five outs away from going to the World Series. The Marlins went on to rally in the game and the series, defeating the Cubs four games to three. Cubs' fans exorcised that bit of Cubs history when the ball was blown up in a tent outside of Harry Caray's restaurant. MSNBC televised the event nationally. A Hollywood special effects expert reduced the ball that came to symbolize the Cubs' cursed history to a pile of thread. Oscar winner Michael Lantieri, who worked on *Jurassic Park* and *Back to the Future,* designed the stunt. He used a combination of pressure, heat and explosives in a bulletproof tank to destroy the ball. In its final hours, the ball was put on display, and steak and lobster were placed in front of it as a "last meal." "I have no intention, whatsoever, of exercising my right to grant clemency or pardon or reprieve," Illinois Governor Rod Blagojevich joked. "That baseball has got to go." Grant DePorter purchased the ball at an auction for $113,824 on behalf of Harry Caray's Restaurant Group, which used the funds for diabetes research.

The question of the Day.

What Cubs batter has the most at bats with the club without hitting a home run?

Jack McCarthy, an outfielder with the Cubs in 1900, and again from 1903 through 1905, holds the distinction with 1,206 at-bats without a homer. Otherwise, he was a fairly solid hitter with a .279 batting average while with the Cubs. Special mention should go to Jimmy Slagle, also an outfielder, who hit just one homer with the Cubs in 3,385 at-bats from 1902 through 1908.

Player, Position	Years with club	At bats
Jack McCarthy, of	1900, 1903–05	1,206
Bill Killefer, c	1918–21	970
Richie Ashburn, of	1960–61	854
Mick Kelleher, inf	1976–80	792
Cupid Childs, 2b	1900–01	767
Guy Bush, p	1923–34	737
Bobby Mattick, ss	1938–40	620
Bobby Lowe, 2b	1902–03	577
Albert Spalding, p	1876–77	550
Eddie Stanky, 2b	1943–44	535

On this date in 1981 . . .

The Cubs traded Dave Kingman to the Mets for Steve Henderson and cash. In three seasons with the Cubs, Kingman hit .278 with 94 homers in 1,182 at-bats with the Cubs. Unruly and ill mannered, he turned off fans, teammates and the front office with his boorish behavior. Even Pulitzer Prize-winning columnist Mike Royko, a lifelong Cubs fanatic, temporarily became a supporter of the White Sox because of Kingman's churlish character. Royko dubbed him "Ding Dong," a play on Kingman's nickname of "King Long." "I prefer an owner (Bill Veeck) with a wooden leg," wrote Royko, "to a left fielder with a wooden head." On April 3, 1980, Kingman doused 25-year-old Dan Friske of the suburban Arlington Heights *Daily Herald* with a bucket of ice water. Friske was interviewing Lenny Randle in the Cubs' clubhouse. "This will give you something to write about for days," Kingman shouted. Later, he said it was a "joke." In June, Kingman was fined $1,250 for failing to show up for a game. He missed another game in August because of an injured shoulder. Instead, he attended a city festival where he appeared for a fee in a booth to promote the Jet Ski.

March

01 March

Happy Birthday Harry Caray.

Harry Caray was born on this date in 1914. Caray and the Cubs are linked forever in the minds of baseball fans all over the country, but he was with the club for only 16 of the 53 years that he was an announcer of major league games on radio and television. Caray did not move into the Wrigley Field booth until he was 68 years old. Previously, he was the announcer for the Cardinals (1945–1969), Athletics (1970) and White Sox (1971–1981). Jerry Reinsdorf and Eddie Einhorn purchased the White Sox in 1981 and wanted to drastically reduce the number of games offered to fans for free over WGN-TV in favor of airing the games on a subscription basis. Caray bluntly told the two that the plan would not work and was hired by the Cubs. Timing is everything, and the timing for Caray's move from the South Side to the North Side was perfect. WGN was going national with its "Superstation" cable. Caray went from having an audience of 50,000 in Greater Chicago that watched his White Sox broadcasts to having about 28 million viewers on WGN by the end of the 1980s. Late in his life, Caray became a cult figure as fans as far away as Maine, Florida, Utah and Oregon caught the excitement of Cubs baseball, in part because of Caray's exuberant personality.

02 March

The question of the day.

What was the origin of the tradition of singing "Take Me Out to the Ballgame" by Harry Caray and the subsequent "guest conductors" at Wrigley Field?

It began as a practical joke at Comiskey Park in 1976. Like many fans, Caray loved to sing "Take Me Out to the Ballgame" during the seventh inning stretch. And like many fans, Harry sang with a decided lack of musical training. On Opening Day that year, without the announcer's knowledge, Sox owner Bill Veeck had a microphone set up in the booth, and Caray's raspy voice was soon bellowing throughout the ballpark. The fans loved it, and from that day on, Caray's enthusiastic rendering of the song was a Chicago tradition. When Harry moved to Wrigley Field in 1982, the tradition went with him and was soon an eagerly anticipated event by television viewers across the country. WGN-TV did not cut away to a commercial until Caray completed the song.

Happy Birthday Ned Williamson.

Ned Williamson was born on this date in 1857. A third baseman with the Cubs from 1879 through 1889, Williamson was the first player in major league history to hit three home runs in one game. It happened on May 30, 1884, during a 12-2 win over Detroit in Chicago. The absurd dimensions of Lakefront Park, which served as the home of the Cubs in 1883 and 1884, helped Williamson. It had the smallest playing field in major league history. The six-foot high left-field fence was just 180 feet from home plate. The center-field barrier was 300 feet away, and right field was 196 feet, although there was a 20-foot high fence in that direction topped by a 17½-foot tarpaulin to block the view of bystanders on a nearby viaduct. The power alleys were 280 feet to left-center and 252 feet to right-center. In 1883, any ball hit over the fence was a ground rule double. In 1884, balls over the fence were home runs. As a result, the Cubs hit 142 home runs that season, a staggering figure for the period. In 57 home games, the Cubs hit 131 homers and allowed 66. On the road, Chicago hit only 11 home runs in 56 contests, and the pitchers surrendered 17. The 142 homers remained a major league record for a team until the 1927 Yankees hit 158. Williamson hit 27 homers, 25 of them at home.

On this date in 1914 . . .

Charles Weeghman, owner of the Federal League franchise the Chicago Whales, broke ground for Weeghman Park, now known as Wrigley Field. Weeghman was a wealthy Chicago restaurateur, one of the first purveyors of what today is described as "fast food." Previously used by the Chicago Lutheran Theological Seminary, Weeghman chose the site because Chicago's population was moving rapidly north, and fans could easily reach the ballpark on the Milwaukee Road train and the elevated train from the loop. The groundbreaking ceremony attracted over 5,000 people. The ballpark, with about 14,000 seats and 2,000 more in the bleachers, was built in seven weeks with 490 men working around the clock. The architect was Zachary Taylor Davis, who also designed the original Comiskey Park, which opened in 1910. The Whales christened the park by defeating Kansas City 9-1 on April 23, 1914, before 21,000 spectators, many of whom stood behind ropes in the outfield because the stands were packed. The Federal League lasted only two seasons, and the Cubs moved into the facility in 1916. It was known as Weeghman Park until 1918, Cubs Park from 1919 through 1926 and Wrigley Field since 1927.

05 March

The question of the day.

How many different players started in left field on Opening Day for the Cubs in the 12 seasons from 1987 through 1998?

There were 12 in all. Brian Dayett (1987), Rafael Palmeiro (1988), Mitch Webster (1989), Lloyd McClendon (1990), George Bell (1991), Luis Salazar (1992), Candy Maldonado (1993), Derrick May (1994), Scott Bullett (1995), Luis Gonzalez (1996), Brant Brown (1997) and Henry Rodriguez (1998) all played the position for the Cubs. Seasonal team leaders in games started in left over the same period were Jerry Mumphrey (1987), Palmeiro (1988), Dwight Smith (1989 and 1990), Bell (1991), May (1992, 1993 and 1994), Gonzalez (1995 and 1996), Doug Glanville (1997) and Rodriguez (1998).

06 March

On this date in 1987 . . .

The Cubs signed Andre Dawson as a free agent. Many considered Dawson to be the top player in baseball during the early 1980s, but over time playing on the artificial surface at Olympic Stadium while on the Expos' roster ravaged his knees. He hoped to extend his baseball career by playing on the grass at Wrigley Field. In a successful publicity coup, Dawson's agent Dick Moss advised him to go to the Cubs' Arizona camp and offer his services at a discount. General manager Dallas Green was unhappy that Dawson was in Mesa and publicly complained about the outfielder's presence. Green could not disclose the real reason for his refusal to sign Dawson. Some months earlier, major league owners secretly agreed not to sign each other's free agents. The Cubs also already had a right fielder in Keith Moreland. When the stalemate between Dawson and the Cubs continued, Moss told Green he would submit a blank contract. Green finally gave in and signed Dawson for $500,000, which made him the 15th highest paid player on the club. The Cubs didn't regret the decision. Moreland moved to third base, and Dawson won the National League Most Valuable Player Award in 1987 and was the club's starting right fielder for six years.

The question of the day.

What is the official name of Wrigley Field's bleachers?

The Cubs announced in 2006 that the remodeled bleacher section would be known as the Bud Light Bleachers. It was the first time that a part of Wrigley Field was sold to a corporate sponsor. During the 2005–2006 off-season, the club removed a part of the outer brick wall of the bleachers, which was one of the last vestiges of the 1914 structure. The supporting structure for the new bleachers was encased in a wall of new bricks reminiscent of the original wall, making the sidewalks along Sheffield and Waveland a few feet narrower. Ivy also was planted on the exterior walls. A large luxury suite, fronted by darkened, slanted windows so as not to interfere with the batter's sight lines, occupied the upper part of the formerly vacant center-field area. The juniper bushes, which had previously served as a hitter's backdrop, were removed. Four rows of new juniper bushes were placed in front of the luxury suites. Speaker poles were placed at the back of the bleachers, to the consternation of some of the owners of the rooftop bleachers because the poles were in the path of the view of the playing field. Another notable change was replacing the solid door in the right-field corner with a chain link fence to allow passers-by to see part of the ball field.

On this date in 1996 . . .

Bill Nicholson, a Cub outfielder from 1939 through 1948, died. Nicknamed "Swish" for his mighty swings, Nicholson hit 195 home runs for the Cubs. He led the NL in homers and RBIs in both 1943 and 1944. July 23, 1944, was Nicholson's best day in the majors when he hit four home runs and was given an intentional walk with the bases loaded during a double-header against the Giants in New York. The Cubs won the first game 7-4 but lost the second 12-10. In the opener, Nicholson walked in the second inning, and then went deep in the fourth, sixth and eighth. Combined with the home run he hit in his last plate appearance the previous game against the Giants on July 22, Nicholson homered in four consecutive official at-bats. He is the only player in Cubs history to accomplish the feat. In game two on July 23, Nicholson went long again in the seventh inning. When he came to bat again in the eighth with the bases loaded and two out, Giant player-manager Mel Ott ordered pitcher Andy Hansen to walk Nicholson intentionally to force in a run. The strategy worked because Andy Pafko flied out to end the inning. Adding to the drama, Nicholson and Ott were battling for the NL home run leadership. Each finished with 21 home runs.

09 March

The question of the day.

What major league team wore the first sleeveless jerseys?

The Cubs were the first in 1940. From 1938 through 1942, P. K. Wrigley experimented with different uniform combinations and delegated the marketing staff from his gum company to design the jerseys. As a result, the Cubs had the gaudiest uniforms in the big leagues. The club was also the first team to use zippers on the shirts instead of buttons. A brighter "electric" blue replaced the standard navy blue color, and the thin embroidered piping was swapped for thick stripes. Three red stripes were placed on the forearms of the blue undershirts. In 1941, the team unveiled a new powder blue road uniform, which was quite a change from the traditional gray ones. When Braves manager Casey Stengel saw them for the first time, he asked, "Doesn't the club offer perfume with those uniforms?" Baseball uniforms of the period were of loose-fitting flannel to absorb perspiration and allow for maximum movement. The Cubs' uniforms during the early 1940s, however, were skintight. "No wonder we're in sixth place," complained outfielder Lou Novikoff in 1942. "We look so skinny and weak to other clubs they convince themselves they can blow us over."

10 March

On this date in 1933 . . .

An earthquake jolted the Cubs while they were in spring training in Los Angeles. The quake struck at 5:55 p.m. and resulted in the deaths of 120 people. Earlier in the day, the Cubs lost an exhibition game to the Giants 5-3. The Cubs were at the Biltmore Hotel along with players from the Giants when the earthquake shook the city. Most of the Cubs were in the upper floors of the hotel dressing for dinner. A few frightened players spent the night in the clubhouse at the Los Angeles ballpark, believing it was safer than the hotel. During a 4-1 win over the Giants the following day, aftershocks continued at frequent intervals. At one point, players from both teams huddled around second base as the steel stands of the ballpark swayed.

On this date in 2005 . . .

The Cubs placed plastic netting underneath the lower grandstand at Wrigley Field to guard against falling concrete. Over a six-week period in June and July of 2004, three chunks of concrete fell from the upper deck, a reminder that the stadium is nearly a century old. One piece just missed hitting a five-year-old boy. Chicago Mayor Richard Daley threatened to close down sections of the ballpark if the Cubs failed to adequately address the problem. Heavy mesh netting was placed under the upper deck to protect fans. Although the plastic barrier was considered a better solution than the loose netting put up in 2004 as a temporary fix, there remained a number of spots where crumbling concrete could still be a concern. However, since then, an engineering firm hired by the Cubs deemed the ballpark safe for fans.

The question of the day.

Why were the Cubs nicknamed the "Remnants" in 1901?

The club was nicknamed the "Remnants" because of the many players lost to the newly formed American League, which formally organized on January 28, 1901, as a second major league. The AL also announced plans to raid the National League rosters by offering more lucrative salaries. One of the teams in the new venture was the Chicago White Sox. Not only would the Cubs have to compete with a second major league club for fan patronage in Chicago, but they also felt the strain of the loss of six regulars, a promising youngster and the AL's higher payroll as well. Pitcher Clark Griffith signed a contract with the Sox as a player-manager. Pitcher Nixey Callahan and outfielder Sam Mertes also went to the Sox. Third baseman Bill Bradley and outfielder Jack McCarthy signed deals with the Indians, pitcher Ned Garvin inked a deal with Milwaukee and catcher Roger Bresnahan moved to Baltimore to play for the Orioles. Both Griffith and Bresnahan were future Hall of Famers. The Cubs lost five more regulars to the AL between the 1901 and 1902 seasons in Danny Green, Topsy Hartsel, Tom Hughes, Mike Kahoe and Barry McCormick. The bleeding finally ended in January 1903 when the two leagues agreed to respect each other's contracts.

13 March

The question of the day.

When was the trademark ivy planted at Wrigley Field?

The idea for the ivy adorning the walls of Wrigley Field was a collaboration between P. K. Wrigley and Bill Veeck, Jr. as part of the renovation of the bleachers, which began in 1937. At the time, Veeck was a 23-year-old front office employee. Wrigley instructed him to create a woodsy motif that suggested a "park" and not a "stadium." Veeck planned to plant the ivy after the end of the 1937 season so it would be in full bloom by the following spring. But Wrigley called him just before the last home game of the season to say that he invited people to the park to see the new ivy. Veeck sprung into action and purchased 350 Japanese bittersweet plants and 200 Boston ivy plants from a North Side nursery. Veeck and the grounds crew ran copper wire up the wall and laced the bittersweet with the ivy. Light bulbs were strung along the wall so they could work all night. By morning, the bleacher wall was entirely covered with bittersweet. In time, the ivy took over, becoming a celebrated ornament of the field.

14 March

The question of the day.

How many major league parks have been named Wrigley Field?

There have been two. The other one was in Los Angeles. It was used by the Los Angeles Angels, a minor league team in the Pacific Coast League, from 1925 through 1957 and as a major league facility for the Los Angeles Angels in 1961, the first year of that franchise's existence. In addition to owning the Cubs, William Wrigley, Jr. was also the owner of the original Angels. In 1925, Wrigley built Wrigley Field in Los Angeles. P. K. Wrigley inherited the Angels from his father in 1932 and sold the club to Brooklyn Dodgers owner Walter O'Malley in February 1957. In October of that year, O'Malley announced he was moving the Dodgers to Los Angeles, and the minor league Angels passed out of existence. In 1961, the American League expanded from eight teams to ten and created a new franchise in Los Angeles, also named the Angels. The new team played one season at Wrigley Field. The Angels played at Dodger Stadium from 1962 through 1965 and moved to Anaheim in 1966. Wrigley Field was demolished in 1966 and a city park, which includes a baseball diamond, was created on the site.

The question of the day.

Why did Charlie Grimm place a golf tee in his mouth during spring training in 1925?

Grimm and teammate Rabbit Maranville teamed up for a classic gag photo. Grimm lay on his back with a golf tee holding a ball clenched between his teeth. Above him was Maranville, a golf club poised in his backswing ready for a follow-through. After the picture was snapped, Maranville suddenly swung the club and knocked the ball down the fairway, frightening the wits out of Grimm.

Happy Birthday Hee-Seop Choi.

Hee-Seop Choi was born on this date in 1979. He signed with the Cubs in 1998 when he was a member of the South Korean national team after being discovered by Cubs scout Leon Lee. Choi made the Cubs roster as a first baseman in 2002. His career took a turn for the worse when he suffered a severe concussion in a violent collision with Kerry Wood during a 5-2 win over the Yankees at Wrigley Field on June 7, 2003. In the fifth inning, Jason Giambi hit an infield pop-up. Choi and Wood both reached for it, and Wood's glove hit Choi in the face. The first baseman fell hard, slamming the back of his head on the ground. Choi was motionless for several minutes and was taken off the field in an ambulance. He was traded to the Marlins for Derrek Lee on November 25, 2003, in what has proven to be one of the greatest trades in club history. Ironically, Derrek is the son of Leon Lee. In 2003, Leon became the first African American manager in Japanese baseball history as the skipper of the Orix BlueWave.

On this date in 1966 . . .

William Shlensky, who owned two shares of stock in the Cubs, filed suit against P. K. Wrigley and all members of the board of directors to force the Cubs to play night baseball at Wrigley Field. Shlensky's suit contended that the Cubs' afternoon games resulted in decreased attendance, the loss of concession income and limited radio and television audiences that inhibited management from "making expenditures for new player development and new player acquisition." Shlensky lost his suit in the Illinois Appellate Court in a 3-0 decision in March 1968.

Happy Birthday Hi Bithorn.

Hi Bithorn was a pitcher for the Cubs in 1942 and 1943, and after two years in the service during World War II, again in 1946 and 1947. He had a record of 18-12 with a 2.60 ERA and seven shutouts in 1943. Hiram Gabriel Bithorn was born in San Juan, Puerto Rico, on March 18, 1916, although both of his parents were Dutch. He was the first Puerto Rican–born player to reach the major leagues. After the 1943 season, Bithorn entered the U.S. Navy, and during his two years in the military his weight ballooned from 180 pounds to 225. He was never effective after the war and drifted to the Mexican League. A policeman shot Bithorn to death under mysterious circumstances on December 30, 1951, in El Mante, Mexico. The ballpark in San Juan is named Hiram Bithorn Stadium in honor of the former Cubs pitcher. The Montreal Expos played a portion of their schedule there in 2003 and 2004.

On this date in 1965 . . .

Cubs broadcaster Jack Quinlan died in an auto accident near Mesa, Arizona, at age 38. He had been in the WGN radio booth since 1956. He was killed driving to the Cubs' team hotel after playing a round of golf in Chandler, Arizona. Quinlan lost control of the rented vehicle and skidded some 100 feet into a parked semi-trailer. Since 1967, the annual Jack Quinlan Memorial Golf Tournament has been held to benefit the Boys and Girls Club of Chicago.

On this date in 1954 . . .

The Cubs traded Roy Smalley to the Braves for Dave Cole and cash. Smalley had been a constant source of frustration for Cubs fans since his rookie year in 1948. He had solid power for a shortstop with 61 homers in 2,644 at-bats, but his lifetime batting average was only .227. He struck out frequently, leading the league in that category in 1950. Defensively, Smalley had great range, but an unreliable arm. During the 1950s, the Cubs' double play combination was derisively referred to as "Miksis to Smalley to Addison Street." In the three seasons he played in more than 100 games at shortstop, Smalley led the NL in errors. In 1950 he became the only Cub in history to join the "20-50" club: 21 home runs and 51 errors. No major leaguer has committed 50 errors in a season since then. Smalley married Jolene Mauch, the sister of Cubs teammate Gene Mauch, in 1950. Roy and Jolene's son, also named Roy, played in the majors as a shortstop from 1975 through 1987. Among the younger Smalley's managers was his Uncle Gene from 1976 through 1980 with the Twins.

21
March

On this date in 1943 . . .

The Cubs opened spring training camp in French Lick, Indiana. During World War II, teams had to train north of the Ohio River and east of the Mississippi to save on travel expenses. The Cubs shared the French Lick facility with the White Sox. A diamond was laid out between the practice fairway and the parallel 18th fairway of the golf course adjoining the elegant French Lick Springs Hotel. The Cubs trained at French Lick in 1943, 1944 and 1945.

22
March

Happy Birthday Dick Ellsworth.

Dick Ellsworth, who played for the Cubs in 1958 and from 1960 through 1966, was born on this day in 1940. He is the youngest pitcher in Cubs history, making his major league debut at age 18 on June 22, 1958. Ellsworth lasted only through the third inning of a 6-2 loss to the Reds in Cincinnati and did not pitch another big-league game until 1960. He entered the 1963 season with a lifetime record of 26-45. In 1962, Ellsworth was 9-20 with a 5.09 ERA. In a remarkable reversal, he had a terrific season in 1963 with a 22-10 record, a 2.11 ERA, 19 complete games and 185 strikeouts in 290⅔ innings. Dick was only 23, but the heavy workload likely ruined a potentially fine career. From 1964 through 1966, he was 36-55 for the Cubs with an ERA of 3.85. The Cubs traded Ellsworth to the Phillies following the 1966 season, and he finished his career in 1971 with an overall record of 115-137.

On this date in 1967 . . .

Leo Durocher's pal Frank Sinatra watched the Cubs lose 2-1 to the California Angels in an exhibition game in Palm Springs, California. Sinatra sat next to Durocher on a folding chair next to the Cubs dugout. Durocher lived in a Beverly Hills mansion and hobnobbed with the Hollywood crowd. Leo counted Sinatra, Bob Hope, Dean Martin, Jimmy Durante, George Raft and George Jessel among his friends. For a time, Durocher was married to actress Laraine Day.

The question of the day.

What was the "Snub the Cubs" campaign?

In July 1980, Chicago radio station WCFL announced plans for a "Snub the Cubs" event, urging fans to boycott the game against the Astros on August 29 at Wrigley Field. "The idea was to protest the amazing ineptitude of the players and front office," explained broadcaster Chuck Swirsky. "We've had 35 years of awful baseball by the Cubs, and the time has come to stage some sort of demonstration." The plans for the "Snub the Cubs" day were canceled when general manager Bob Kennedy threatened legal action. Swirsky was later the public address announcer for Chicago Bulls games from 1980 to 1983. He also did play-by-play for DePaul University basketball and for the Toronto Raptors. He returned to Chicago in 2008 as the radio announcer for the Bulls.

The question of the day.

What former Chicago Bears player was ejected from Wrigley Field?

Ex-Chicago Bear Steve McMichael sang "Take Me Out to the Ballgame" during the seventh inning stretch of a 5-4 win over the Rockies on August 7, 2001, and publicly berated umpire Angel Hernandez. In the sixth inning, Hernandez called Ron Coomer out at home on a close play. With an open mike at his disposal, McMichael told fans "not to worry" about the call because he would "have some speaks with that umpire after the game." Hernandez tossed McMichael out of the ballpark, and the Cubs apologized profusely.

On this date in 1984 . . .

The Cubs traded Bill Campbell and Mike Diaz to the Phillies for Gary Matthews, Bob Dernier and Porfi Altamirano. The club made a brilliant deal, filling two holes in the outfield at a minimal cost, as Dernier became the starter in center field and Matthews in left. It also had a ripple effect on the rest of the lineup and helped propel the Cubs to the NL East crown and to their first postseason appearance since 1945. Leon Durham moved from the outfield to his natural position at first base, which benched Bill Buckner. Keith Moreland moved into a platoon situation with Mel Hall in right field. By June, Hall and Buckner were traded in deals that brought Dennis Eckersley and Rick Sutcliffe to the Cubs. To fans, however, it appeared to be yet another rearranging of the deck chairs on a sinking team, which lost 91 games in 1983. During spring training of 1984, the Cubs were awful with a 7-20 record, including an 11-game losing streak. Two fights took place between players on the field. Known as "The Sarge," Matthews served as an inspiration force in the clubhouse with his hustle and gung-ho enthusiasm. During the 1984 season, he hit 14 homers, scored 101 runs, batted .291, drew 103 walks and led the NL in on-base percentage.

27
March

On this date in 1902 . . .

The nickname "Cubs" was coined when an anonymous columnist in the *Chicago Daily News* noted that manager "Frank Selee will devote his strongest efforts on the team work of the new Cubs this year." The "cubs" referred to in the article were young players, such as Joe Tinker, who were playing for the club for the first time. Prior to 1902, the Chicago club had been known by a variety of nicknames including "White Stockings," "Whites," "Silk Stockings," "Black Stockings," "Colts," "Orphans" and "Remnants." Other nicknames that appeared frequently in the Chicago papers between 1902 and 1906 were the "Microbes," due to the many players of small stature, the "Zephyrs," because of the team's location in the Windy City, the "Nationals" and the "Spuds," a reference to team president Charles Murphy and the large Irish contingent on the roster. In 1907, player-manager Frank Chance insisted the media call the club the Cubs and only the Cubs. The nickname was officially recognized during the 1907 World Series when the club issued new coats to the players sporting a large white bear figure on each sleeve. Their uniforms in 1908, both at home and on the road, featured a small brown bear holding a bat inside the letter "C."

28
March

On this date in 1947 . . .

Hall of Famer Johnny Evers died. He played second base for the Cubs from 1902 through 1913 and was also the manager in 1913. Evers became part of the most famous infield in major league history, teaming with shortstop Joe Tinker and first baseman Frank Chance. During the period they played together, the Cubs won National League pennants in 1906, 1907, 1908 and 1910. They won the World Series in 1907 and 1908. From 1906 through 1910, the Cubs were an amazing 530-235, a winning percentage of .693 that is easily the best of any franchise over a five-year period since 1900. No team since 1970 has put together a five-year winning percentage better than .626. Evers and Tinker were not on speaking terms off the field, however. The break occurred in 1905 when Evers left for an exhibition game in Bedford, Indiana, in a taxi and left his teammates behind. Later that afternoon, Evers and Tinker engaged in a fistfight on the field. Both had reconciled by the time they were elected together to the Hall of Fame in 1945.

29 March

On this date in 1954 . . .

The Cubs fired manager Phil Cavarretta only 15 days before Opening Day. The Cubs had a record of 5-15 in exhibition games. Asked by P. K. Wrigley for an assessment of the club's chances for improving on their 65-89 record of 1953, Cavarretta gave the owner the plain, unvarnished facts and stated the club's chances of posting a winning record was almost non-existent. "The material just isn't there," said Cavarretta. "What makes it sadder is that the future is even worse. There just isn't any good talent coming up." In Cavarretta's estimation, Ernie Banks, Dale Talbot and Gene Baker were the only young stars capable of making an impact, and Baker was 29 years old. Wrigley stunned Cavarretta by firing him. "Phil seems to have a defeatist attitude," said Wrigley. "We don't believe he should continue in a job where he doesn't believe success is possible." A few days later, Cavarretta signed a contract as a player with the White Sox as a back-up first baseman and pinch-hitter. He remained with the Sox until early in the 1955 season and never managed in the majors again. Under Stan Hack, Cavarretta's replacement, the Cubs were 64-90 in 1954 and finished in seventh place.

30 March

On this date in 1992 . . .

The Cubs traded George Bell to the White Sox for Sammy Sosa and Ken Patterson. It did not look like a great deal at the time, but the Cubs struck gold with this transaction. Bell was still a productive hitter in 1992, while Sosa was a struggling youngster who seemed to be regressing in his development. In 1991, with the White Sox, Sosa hit only .203 with 10 homers in 316 at-bats and struck out 98 times while drawing only 14 walks. He was only 23 when the Cubs acquired him, however, and he became one of the best players of his generation. Bell played only two seasons after being traded away by the Cubs, mostly as a designated hitter. As a Cub, Sosa is the all-time record holder in home runs (545) and is second in slugging percentage (.569), third in RBIs (1,414), fourth in total bases (3,980), sixth in runs (1,245), sixth in walks (748), eighth in at-bats (6,990), ninth in hits (1,985) and 10th in games (1,811). He holds single season club records in home runs (66 in 1998), slugging percentage (.737 in 2001), total bases (425 in 2001) and extra base hits (103 in 2001).

31
March

On this date in 2003 . . .

Corey Patterson set a Cubs record for most runs batted in on Opening Day with seven during a 15-2 drubbing of the Mets at Shea Stadium. Hitting seventh in the lineup, Patterson singled in a run off Tom Glavine in the first inning and collected another RBI-single facing Glavine in the third. Patterson later hit two home runs against Mike Bacsik, with two men on base in the sixth and one on in the seventh. Mark Grudzielanek was 3-for-3 in his Cubs debut, and Mark Bellhorn drove in four runs. Reliever Juan Cruz struck out six batters in a row in the sixth and seventh.

Wrigley Hits 100

April

01 April

On this date in 1997 . . .

The Cubs lost on Opening Day 4-2 to the Marlins in Miami and began the longest losing streak in Cubs history. On April 4, the Cubs played the first ever game at Turner Field in Atlanta and were defeated 5-4 to fall to 0-4. The Cubs dropped to 0-7 with a 5-3 loss to the Marlins in their home opener on April 8. Defeat number eight was a 1-0 decision to the Marlins at Wrigley Field in which the Cubs' only hit off Alex Fernandez was a single by Dave Hansen with one out in the ninth inning. The club received a bit of a reprieve when the April 11 clash against the Braves was postponed by a Chicago snowstorm. The 11th straight loss happened on April 15 by a 10-7 score against the Rockies at Wrigley Field. The 13th defeat in a row was on April 19, 6-3 to the Mets in New York. The losing pitcher was Turk Wendell, who wore number 13. During a double-header at Shea Stadium on April 20, the Cubs lost their 14th in succession 8-2, and then broke the skid in the second tilt, winning 4-3. That victory was not easy, with the Mets scoring twice in the ninth. The Cubs teams in 1944, 1982 and 1985 lost 13 in a row. The only major league team with a worse start was the 1988 Orioles, who were 0-22.

02 April

The question of the day.

When was the basket installed near the top of the outfield wall at Wrigley Field?

The basket was installed during the 1970 season. A rash of fights and general unruly behavior brought about changes at Wrigley Field that season. Video cameras were installed so that every area of the ballpark could be scanned for trouble spots. It was the first use of cameras at any park in baseball. They put the baskets in place in response to fans throwing debris onto the field and reaching over the wall to interfere with batted balls. There was also a problem with inebriated fans jumping off the wall and onto the playing field. Others, trying to walk across the top of the wall, fell to the warning track below. In response, the 42-inch mesh screen was constructed around the front wall of the bleachers. It was fastened 30 inches below the top of the wall and angled at 45 degrees. The screen shortened the home run distance at Wrigley by three feet.

03
April

On this date in 1987 . . .

The Cubs traded future Hall of Famer Dennis Eckersley to the Athletics for Dan Wilder, who never appeared in a big-league game. At the time the deal was completed, Eckersley was 32 years old and had a lifetime record of 151-128. Most of his success came early in his career with the Indians and Red Sox, and he had not won more than 13 games in a season since 1979. During the 1986 campaign with the Cubs, Eckersley pitched in 33 games, 32 of them starts, and had a record of 6-11 with an ERA of 4.57. The lone relief appearance was his first in 10 years. Oakland manager Tony LaRussa saw potential in Eckersley out of the bullpen, however, and it proved to be one of the best decisions in baseball history. From 1988 through 1992, Eckersley pitched 359⅔ innings and had an ERA of 1.90. He allowed 247 hits and walked only 38 with 378 strikeouts. Over those five remarkable seasons, Eckersley's won-lost record was 24-7, and he recorded 220 saves. While the trade has to rank with the worst in Cubs history, it is open to question whether Gene Michael, who managed the Cubs in 1987, or Don Zimmer, who was skipper from 1988 through 1991, would have possessed the foresight to convert Eckersley from a struggling starter into a dominant closer.

04
April

On this date in 1994 . . .

Cubs outfielder Karl "Tuffy" Rhodes hit three home runs in his first three at-bats on Opening Day, although the Cubs lost 12-8 to the Mets. A 22-mile an hour wind blowing toward the ivy-covered walls helped Rhodes. Batting leadoff, Rhodes homered in the first, third and fifth innings, each of them off Dwight Gooden. Rhodes also walked in the sixth and singled in the ninth. The only other player in major league history with three home runs on Opening Day is George Bell of the Blue Jays in 1988. Rhodes is the only one to do it in his first three at-bats, however. Entering the 1994 season, he had only five home runs in 280 big-league at-bats and a .232 batting average while playing for the Astros and Cubs. Following his Opening Day explosion, Rhodes returned to obscurity. He had another 306 at-bats in the big leagues, with just five more homers while compiling a batting average of only .206. Rhodes went to Japan where he became a legitimate home run hitter. In 2001 with the Kinetsu Buffaloes, Rhodes smacked 55 home runs to tie the single season Japanese League record set by Sadaharu Oh in 1964.

05
April

The question of the day.

Who is the only First Lady to throw out the ceremonial first pitch at Wrigley Field?

Hillary Clinton is the only First Lady to throw out the first pitch, and it happened on April 4, 1994, in the same game that Karl Rhodes homered in his first three at-bats. Wearing a blue Cubs blazer and a baseball cap, Hillary threw from the first row of seats on the third base side. She also sang "Take Me Out to the Ballgame" with Harry Caray during the seventh inning stretch and smooched the legendary broadcaster at the conclusion of the duet. Her husband Bill threw out the first pitch on the same day in Cleveland at the first game ever played at Jacobs Field. From Cleveland, the President flew to Charlotte, North Carolina, to cheer the University of Arkansas basketball team to a 76-72 win over Duke in the NCAA championship game.

06
April

Happy Birthday Phil Regan.

Phil Regan, a relief pitcher for the Cubs from 1968 through 1972, was born on this date in 1937. Many accused Regan of using foreign substances on the ball, and the issue came to a head on August 18, 1968, during a 6-3 loss to the Reds. In the seventh inning, umpire Chris Pelakoudas went to the mound and inspected Regan's cap. He claimed he found Vaseline on the inside of the cap. When the game resumed, Pelakoudas charged Regan with throwing three illegal pitches "by watching the break on the ball." The ump nullified a fly ball and a strikeout and changed a strike call to a ball. After the strikeout was reversed, Pete Rose hit a single. The 30,942 in attendance booed loudly and threw debris onto the field. Manager Leo Durocher and players Randy Hundley and Al Spangler were all thrown out of the game. Regan, surprisingly, was allowed to remain in the contest. The Cubs protested the defeat. After a special hearing on August 20, NL President Warren Giles disallowed the protest but said in the future umpires should have better evidence before ruling a pitch illegal. Trying to find an illegal substance on Regan's person became a Holy Grail for NL umpires, however; games were often stopped for inspections. The frisking ceased in 1971 when Regan stopped pitching effectively.

07 April

On this date in 1988 . . .

The Cubs installed the first lights at Wrigley Field. It began when a helicopter lifted the first steel girders to workmen on the roof of the upper deck. Six 33-foot towers were erected; three down the left-field line and three in right. The latticework of the towers was designed to mirror the vintage architecture of the park. General Electric of Hendersonville, North Carolina, built the lighting system at a cost of $5 million. There were no light towers placed in the bleacher area between the left-field foul pole and the right-field foul pole. "We designed the lights," said Cubs President Donald Grenesko, "so you could sit in the grandstand and look out at the field and feel nothing had changed."

08 April

On this date in 1960 . . .

The Cubs made one of their worst trades sending Ron Perranoski, John Goryl, Lee Handley and $25,000 to the Dodgers for Don Zimmer. Zimmer was 29 years old and coming off a season in which he hit .165 as a utility infielder, yet the Cubs saw fit to trade three prospects and cash to the Dodgers to obtain his services. Perranoski had a 10-year run of success as one of the premier relief pitchers in baseball with both the Dodgers and the Twins. In addition, Zimmer was acquired to play third base even though Ron Santo was about to take over the position, and Frank Thomas would have been a better option in the meantime. They later moved Zimmer to second base. The Cubs dealt Tony Taylor to the Phillies to make room for Zimmer at second in another poorly conceived trade.

09 *April*

On this date in 1983 . . .

Cubs pitcher Dickie Noles was arrested following a tavern brawl in Cincinnati. He was charged with assault, resisting arrest and disorderly conduct. Besides being fined by the Cubs, Noles was named in a $500,000 civil suit by one of the arresting police officers and a $300,000 suit by the doorman at the bar. When the pitcher appeared in court in Cincinnati on July 6, he entered a plea of no contest. The judge sentenced Noles to 180 days in jail but suspended 150 days. Noles was also credited with the 14 days he spent at Chicago's Northwestern Memorial Hospital, where he had undergone treatment for alcohol addiction at the club's insistence. Shortly after the season ended, Noles served the remainder of his 16-day jail sentence in Cincinnati. At the same time, he donated $1,000 to the Greater Cincinnati Knothole Baseball League. Noles later worked for the Phillies and Major League Baseball, traveling the minor leagues to counsel players on the dangers of alcohol and drugs.

10 *April*

On this date in 1962 . . .

The Cubs participated in the first ever major league game played in the state of Texas and lost 11-2 to the Colts at Colt Stadium in Houston. The Cubs lost all three games of the series, dropping the last two by identical 2-0 scores. One of the pitchers that shut out the Cubs was Dean Stone, who was pitching in his first big-league game in three years. The Cubs ended the season with a record of 59-103 and finished behind the Houston expansion club, which was 64-96. During the first three years of their existence, the Houston franchise was officially known as the "Colt .45s" and informally as the "Colts." The nickname was changed to "Astros" in 1965. Houston played for three years at Colt Stadium, a temporary facility built in what would become the parking lot for the Astrodome, baseball's first domed stadium, which opened in 1965. The Cubs played indoors for the first time on April 30, 1965, and lost 4-3. The Cubs had a more than two-decade-long stretch of futility in Houston. From 1962 through 1986, the club was 55-115 in the city.

11 April

The question of the day.

Has anyone hit the Wrigley Field scoreboard with a batted ball during a regular-season game? No, but two have come close. Bill Nicholson of the Cubs hit a drive off Al Brazle of the Cardinals during a 6-2 win on April 24, 1948, which passed the right side of the scoreboard, struck a building and bounced off the hood of a southbound car on Sheffield Avenue. Roberto Clemente nearly hit the left side of the Wrigley Field scoreboard with a long home run during a 7-6 Pirates win over the Cubs on May 17, 1959. Clemente clobbered a Bob Henry pitch in the ninth inning. The hit was estimated to have traveled 500 feet. Legendary golfer Sam Snead did hit the scoreboard with a golf ball before a game on April 18, 1952. Snead teed off from home plate.

12 April

Happy Birthday Walt Moryn.

A power-hitting outfielder with the Cubs from 1952 through 1956, Walt Moryn was born on this date in 1926. He had a tremendous day on May 30, 1958, in a Memorial Day double-header against the Dodgers at Wrigley Field. In the opener, the Cubs scored three runs in the ninth inning to win 3-2. Moryn drove in the tying run with a two-out double and scored the winning run on Sammy Taylor's single. In the second tilt, Moryn clouted three home runs, the third a ninth inning walk-off blast, for a 10-8 Cubs win. The Dodgers led 7-1 when Ernie Banks and Moryn hit back-to-back homers off Don Newcombe. Moryn and Chuck Tanner clubbed consecutive home runs off Ed Roebuck in the seventh to tie the score 8-8. Moryn's game-winner in the ninth was hit off Sandy Koufax with a man on base.

The question of the day.

Who won the National League Most Valuable Player Award in 1952?

Cubs outfielder Hank Sauer was the MVP in 1952 on a club that posted a record of 77-77. In the first 51 games of the season, he hit .359 and had 18 homers and 58 RBIs. Sauer finished the campaign by batting .270 with league-leading totals in home runs (37) and runs batted in (121). He came to the Cubs in a June 15, 1949, trade with the Reds along with Frank Baumholtz for Harry Walker and Peanuts Lowrey. It was one of the best deals in club history, as Sauer hit 198 homers for the Cubs through 1955. After each homer at Wrigley Field, fans in the bleachers threw packages of Hank's favorite chewing tobacco onto the field. What he could not stuff in his pockets, he stashed in the vines. Sauer's slugging percentage of .512 is the fifth highest of any Cub with at least 2,000 plate appearances, trailing only Hack Wilson, Sammy Sosa, Aramis Ramirez and Derrek Lee.

On this date in 1976 . . .

Dave Kingman hit the longest home run in Wrigley Field history. It was accomplished while playing for the Mets during a 6-5 Cubs victory. The drive carried 550 feet over Waveland Avenue, and after bouncing a few times, struck the side of a house three doors down on the east side of Kenmore Avenue. The residents of the house poured onto the front porch to see what was knocking at their wall. Kingman hit the same house when he was playing for the Cubs on May 17, 1979, with a drive off Ron Reed. The only player to ever put a ball on a rooftop beyond Wrigley Field was Glenallen Hill of the Cubs during a 14-8 loss to the Brewers in a game that lasted four hours and 22 minutes without going to extra innings. Hill's drive landed on a rooftop across Waveland.

On this day in 1941 . . .

The Cubs won an eventful Opening Day with a 7-4 decision over the Pirates at Wrigley Field. Claude Passeau was the winning pitcher, despite nearly being knocked out in the first inning. Pittsburgh leadoff batter Frankie Gustine smacked a line drive that struck Passeau on the knee. There was a five-minute delay in the game before Passeau was able to resume pitching. The Cubs had four rookies in the starting lineup in catcher Clyde McCullough, first baseman Eddie Waitkus, left fielder Lou Novikoff and shortstop Lou Stringer. All but McCullough, who played in nine games in 1940, were making their big-league debuts. It was not a good day for the 23-year-old Stringer. Although he had three hits, including two doubles, Stringer made four errors. In four years in the minors, he played exclusively at second base, but future Hall of Famer Billy Herman was firmly entrenched at the position. Opening Day in 1941 was Stringer's first regular-season game at shortstop during his professional career. Stringer played seven games at short for the Cubs before he was moved back to his natural position at second base after the Cubs traded Herman on May 6. Stringer led all NL second baseman in assists in 1941.

On this date in 1898 . . .

Officials stopped a game between the Cubs and Cardinals when a fire broke out at Sportsman's Park in St. Louis. The ballpark was crowded with 6,000 people when the flames were discovered in the second inning. The players on both teams did heroic work rescuing many fans as the fire, fueled by strong winds, spread rapidly. At least 100 were burned and many suffered broken limbs from jumping from the stands to the ground. The flames destroyed the ballpark along with the saloon and residence of Cardinals owner Chris Von Der Ahe. It also damaged an adjacent railway depot and the fairgrounds across the street. A lit cigar carelessly placed on the tarpaulins was the suspected cause. Von Der Ahe ordered his manager Tim Hurst and his players to work all night clearing debris from the fire and to help carpenters erect 1,700 temporary seats. The following day, the Cubs scored 10 runs in the fourth inning and defeated the exhausted St. Louis club 14-1.

17 April

On this date in 1976 . . .

Mike Schmidt hit four home runs and drove in eight runs as the Phillies rallied from an 11-run deficit to defeat the Cubs 18-16 in 10 innings at Wrigley Field. The Cubs scored seven runs in the second inning off Steve Carlton and led 12-1 after three innings and 13-2 after four. The Phillies scored two runs in the fifth inning on Schmidt's first homer off Rick Reuschel. They added three more in the seventh, one on Schmidt's second home run, again facing Rick Reuschel. Philadelphia scored five in the eighth, three on Schmidt's third home run, this time against Paul Reuschel. In the ninth inning, the Phillies scored three times to pull ahead 15-13. After giving up 13 unanswered runs, the Cubs finally plated two runs, tying the score 15-15 on a two-out single by Steve Swisher. In the 10th, Schmidt tied a major league record for most home runs in a game by hitting his fourth of the day, a two-run shot off Darold Knowles over the center-field fence to make the score 17-15. Each club added one more run to make the final 18-16. Through 2008, only 15 players have hit four homers in a game. Schmidt is one of two to accomplish the feat against the Cubs. The other was Ed Delahanty of the Phillies on July 13, 1896, in Chicago.

18 April

Happy Birthday Danny Friend.

A pitcher with the Cubs from 1895 through 1898, Danny Friend was born on this day in 1873. He was involved in a wild afternoon in New York on August 30, 1897, in which he appeared in a game wearing a bathrobe. With the Cubs leading 7-5 at the end of the eighth inning, player-manager Cap Anson was fined $25 and thumbed by umpire Bob Emslie for arguing that it was too dark to continue the contest. After the Cubs rallied for three runs in the top of the ninth to take a 10-5 lead, left fielder George Decker moved to first base to replace Anson. Friend had already showered and was wearing his street clothes when summoned to play left. Friend donned his Chicago baseball cap, slipped on a bathrobe and trotted onto the field. Giants manager Bill Joyce protested because Friend was out of uniform, and as he and Emslie argued, the umpire decided it was too dark to continue. The top of the ninth was canceled, and the score reverted to a 7-5 Chicago win.

19 April

On this date in 1931 . . .

During a 4-1 Cubs win in St. Louis, an odd call by umpire Charley Evans triggered a protest by the Cardinals. The Cards sold more tickets than seats available, and the overflow was placed behind ropes in the outfield. Chicago left fielder Riggs Stephenson momentarily held a drive by Jim Bottomley, and then dropped it into the crowd. Evans called Bottomley out, claiming the crowd verbally interfered with Stephenson. The Cards filed a protest with National League President John Heydler, but it was denied.

20 April

On this date in 1916 . . .

The Cubs played their first game at present day Wrigley Field, then known as Weeghman Park. The home team won 7-6 in 11 innings before a crowd of 18,000. The Cubs scored two runs in the eighth and one in the ninth to send the contest into extra innings. The ninth-inning run scored on doubles by Max Flack and Heinie Zimmerman. The winning tally in the 11th came on a double by Cy Williams and a single from Vic Saier. A parade from Grant Park through the downtown streets preceded the game. At the ballpark, flowers were presented to each of the Cubs. Aerial bombs were set up, with each burst releasing American flags that sailed all over the North Side. One of the attractions at Weeghman Park in 1916 was "Joa," a bear cub donated by Cubs minority owner J. Ogden Armour. The name of the cub was derived from Armour's initials. They housed the bear in a cage outside the park on Addison Street.

21 *April*

Happy Birthday Bill Faul.

Pitcher Bill Faul was born on this date in 1940. Purchased from the Tigers in March 1965, Faul was only 7-10 with a 4.07 ERA over two seasons in Chicago, but he will long be remembered as one of the most colorful characters ever to wear a Cubs uniform. Faul was a master hypnotist, a karate instructor in the Air Force, had his hands and feet registered as deadly weapons, held a degree as a Doctor of Divinity, preached for the Universal Christian Church and insisted on wearing uniform number 13. Faul hypnotized himself before each start and claimed it helped him relax and concentrate. To put himself in the trance-like state, Faul would walk off the mound, turn his back on the hitter and wave his hand in front of his face a few times. Faul pitched three shutouts in a span of 27 days in July and August of 1965, and his eccentricities were tolerated as long as he was pitching effectively. Inconsistent performances, however, led to a ticket back to the minors in July 1966. Faul also was involved in a statistical oddity. The 1965 Cubs are one of only six teams since 1900 with three triple plays in a season. All three were pulled off with Faul on the mound, even though he pitched only 96⅔ innings during the season.

22 *April*

On this date in 1934 . . .

Lon Warneke became the only pitcher in Cubs history to throw consecutive one-hitters. The first came on Opening Day on April 17 against the Reds in Cincinnati. Warneke not only surrendered one hit but also struck out 13 in a 6-0 victory. He carried a no-hitter into the ninth inning before Adam Comorosky singled with one out. It was Warneke's second straight shutout in the season opener, following the one he tossed against the Cardinals in 1933. The April 22, 1934, contest resulted in a 15-2 triumph over the Cards in St. Louis. The only hit off Warneke was a double by Ripper Collins in the fifth inning. Warneke finished the season with a 22-10 record, 23 complete games, 291⅓ innings and a 3.21 ERA. He pitched through a severe cold in May and June that caused him to lose 15 pounds. Doctors ordered Warneke to go on a diet of eggs and beer to put the weight back on his frame. From 1932 through 1936, he was 98-58 with the Cubs before the club made the mistake of trading him to the Cardinals. After his playing days, Warneke was a National League umpire from 1949 through 1955. He holds the distinction of both playing in a World Series (1932 and 1935) as well as umpiring in one (1954).

The question of the day.

When was the last time that the White Sox drew more fans than the Cubs?

The last time the White Sox outdrew the Cubs was in 1991 and 1992, the first two years after the second Comiskey Park (now U. S. Cellular Field) opened. The following is a list of which years each club was the Windy City leader in attendance:

Team	Year(s)	Team	Year(s)
White Sox	1901–1902	White Sox	1941
Cubs	1903	Cubs	1942–1950
White Sox	1904–1905	White Sox	1951–1957
Cubs	1906	Cubs	1958
White Sox	1907	White Sox	1959–1967
Cubs	1908–1909	Cubs	1968–1973
White Sox	1910–1917	White Sox	1974
Cubs	1918	Cubs	1975–1980
White Sox	1919–1922	White Sox	1981–1984
Cubs	1923–1924	Cubs	1985–1990
White Sox	1925	White Sox	1991–1992
Cubs	1926–1940	Cubs	1993–2008

On this date in 1938 . . .

Dizzy Dean shut out his former Cardinals teammates 5-0 at Wrigley Field. The Cubs acquired him eight days earlier in a blockbuster deal where the Cubs sent Curt Davis, Clyde Shoun, Tuck Stainback and $185,000 to St. Louis. At the time, with his larger-than-life personality and pitching ability, Dean was among the most well-known individuals in America. From 1932 through 1936, he had a record of 120-65 with the Cardinals, which included a 30-7 season in 1934. He slipped to 13-10 in 1937, however, and was out for most of the second half of the season following an injury suffered in the All-Star Game when Earl Averill lined a pitch off his big toe. Dean came back from the injury too soon and hurt his shoulder. The arm was no doubt weakened by an excessive workload before the toe injury. For five consecutive seasons from 1932 through 1936, Dean averaged 306 innings, 34 starts and 15 relief appearances per season. Dean was 28 years old when he arrived in Chicago, but his arm never fully bounced back from the injury. Over four seasons with the Cubs, he pitched only 225 innings, although he was reasonably effective when healthy with a 16-8 record and a 3.36 ERA.

On this date in 1876 . . .

The Cubs played their first National League game and won 4-0 over the Louisville Grays in Louisville. Albert Spalding pitched the shutout. Spalding was also the manager of the team. The lineup for the first game was Ross Barnes (2b), Cap Anson (3b), Cal McVey (1b), Paul Hines (cf), Spalding (p), Bob Addy (rf), Deacon White (c), Johnny Peters (ss) and John Glenn (lf). Two days later, the Cubs played their second game and won again 10-0 over Louisville with Spalding pitching another shutout. Spalding shut out the opposition so often in the early going in 1876, that when any club was held without a run it was said that they were "Chicagoed." The slang term remained part of baseball's lexicon into the early part of the 20th century. Also in 1876, Spalding and his brother J. Walter opened a large store at 118 Randolph Street, in Chicago, where they sold "all kinds of baseball goods." This was the start of the Spalding sporting goods enterprise. The business was enormously successful, and both Spaldings became millionaires. The company is still the official supplier for balls for the National Basketball Association and the Arena Football League.

The question of the day.

What was the most grueling road trip in Cubs history?

During the 1936 spring training exhibition season, the Cubs endured a brutal coast-to-coast trip that lasted from March 16 through April 9. Over the course of 25 days, the club played in 20 different cities. The Cubs had scheduled games in Los Angeles, San Antonio, Houston and New Orleans. It also included stops in the Florida cities of Pensacola, Tallahassee, Lakeland, Tampa, St. Petersburg, Bradenton, Clearwater, Winter Haven and Sarasota. Next on the list were the Alabama towns of Selma, Dothan, Montgomery and Birmingham in addition to Thomasville, Georgia and Nashville, Tennessee.

On this date in 1902 . . .

Confused 18-year-old Cubs rookie pitcher Jimmy St. Vrain ran to third base after hitting a grounder to Pirates shortstop Honus Wagner. Normally a right-handed batter, St. Vrain had trouble hitting Pittsburgh right-hander Deacon Phillippe and decided to bat left-handed. Unfortunately, St. Vrain lost his bearings batting from an unfamiliar position and ran up the third base line instead of toward first. The astonished Wagner threw him out. The Pirates won the game in Chicago 2-0. The 1902 season was the only one of St. Vrain's career, and he posted a 4-6 record along with a sparkling ERA of 2.08.

On this date in 1906 . . .

The Cubs used football tactics to steal a 1-0 win from the Reds in Chicago. In the ninth inning with the score 0-0, Frank Chance was a base runner on second, and Joe Tinker was on first. Pat Moran grounded to Reds third baseman Jim Delahanty. Delahanty threw to second baseman Miller Huggins to force Tinker out, who in turn tackled Huggins and held him to the ground while Chance rounded third to score the winning run. The Reds protested loudly, but the umpires allowed the play to stand.

On this date in 1983 . . .

Cubs manager Lee Elia delivered his infamous five-minute, profanity-laced tirade against Cubs fans following a 4-3 loss to the Dodgers before a crowd of 9,391 on a Friday afternoon at Wrigley Field. The loss dropped the Cubs record to 5-14. Elia was unable to contain his rage after a fan doused Keith Moreland and Larry Bowa with beer as the Cubs trudged to the clubhouse after the defeat. "The 3,000 fans who have been watching us each day have been very negative and expecting too much," said Elia. "Why don't they rip me instead of the ballplayers? Eighty-five percent of the world is working, but the 15 percent who come out to Wrigley Field have nothing better to do than to heap abuse and criticism on the team. Why don't they go out and look for jobs?" The outburst was caught on tape and replayed on radio and television stations around the country. The 46 "bleeps" in the tape that were used to cover the profanity added to the backlash against Elia. Within four months, he joined the "15 percent" he said were unemployed. The Cubs fired Elia on August 22.

On this date in 1949 . . .

Rocky Nelson of the Cardinals circled the bases for an "inside-the-glove homer" at Wrigley Field. With the Cubs leading 3-2, two out in the ninth and a St. Louis runner on base, Nelson hit a drive to center fielder Andy Pafko. Pafko thought he made the final out of the game with a diving somersault catch off his shoe tops and ran toward the Cubs dugout with the ball, believing the game was over. Second base umpire Al Barlick, in a delayed call, ruled that Pafko had merely trapped it. Pafko, ignoring his teammates' frantic pleas to throw the ball, raced toward the umpire to protest the decision while Nelson hurried around the bases as the ball sat inside Pafko's glove. He finally made a belated throw home when Nelson was only steps away from the plate, and the Cardinal batter was safe with what proved to be the game-winning run. Arguments by the Cubs delayed the game for 10 minutes, and the crowd of 30,775 showed its disapproval by showering the field with debris.

Wrigley Hits 100

May

01
May

On this date in 1880 . . .

The Cubs achieved the first "walk-off" victory in major league history by scoring two runs in the bottom of the ninth inning to beat the Reds 4-3 in the season opener in Cincinnati. Prior to 1880, the bottom half of the last inning was played until there were three outs regardless of the score. At the time, the batting order was determined by a pre-game coin flip. Chicago won the toss and elected to bat last, which set up the game-ending rally. Pitcher Larry Corcoran, playing in his major league debut, started the ninth with a single. Tom Burns reached third on an error that moved Corcoran to third. After Burns stole second, both he and Corcoran scored on Joe Quest's hit. Earlier in the contest, King Kelly hit the first Opening Day home run in Cubs history. Corcoran had a record of 43-14 in 1880, including a 13-game winning streak, led the league in strikeouts with 268 and compiled an ERA of 1.95. He stood five foot five and weighed a mere 120 pounds, but he pitched 536⅓ innings that season. Corcoran played for the Cubs until 1885, when his arm went dead, and compiled a record of 175-85.

02
May

On this date in 1917 . . .

At Weeghman Park in Chicago, Hippo Vaughn of the Cubs and Fred Toney of the Reds combined to hurl the only game in major league history in which neither team collected a hit through the first nine innings. The first hit of the contest occurred when Reds shortstop Larry Kopf hit a Vaughn pitch into right field for a single. Hal Chase flied to right, but Cubs right fielder Cy Williams muffed the easy catch, putting Chase on first and Kopf on third. After Chase stole second, Jim Thorpe chopped a hit a few feet in front of home plate. Vaughn raced in and tried to throw out Kopf coming in from third base, but catcher Art Wilson dropped the throw, giving the Reds a 1-0 lead. The advantage held up in the bottom of the 10th when Toney retired the Cubs without a hit. Both pitchers walked two batters. Vaughn struck out 10 while Toney fanned three.

03 May

On this date in 1901 . . .

The Cubs purchased future Hall of Fame pitcher Rube Waddell from the Pirates. One of the most eccentric players ever to appear in a big-league game, Pittsburgh cut Waddell loose after he jumped the club. According to Waddell biographer Alan H. Levy, the Pirates were so anxious to get rid of Waddell that Cubs owner James Hart was able to purchase him in exchange for a cigar. Waddell pitched his first game with the Cubs on May 5 and lost 4-2 to the Pirates, but the Chicago crowd of 14,000, the largest of the year, cheered him wildly. In his next start, against the Cardinals, Waddell covered first base and was leveled by St. Louis batter Art Nichols. Rube popped up from the collision and turned somersaults on his way back to the mound. Crowds in Chicago continued to be much larger than normal on days that Waddell pitched in 1901, but after posting a 14-14 record, he left the Cubs in August, claiming he was going fishing, and he never returned. In September, Waddell pitched for semi-pro clubs in Gray's Lake, Wisconsin, and Burlington, Illinois. He signed a contract with the Philadelphia Athletics in 1902 and had a record of 97-52 from that season through 1905. Waddell was elected to the Hall of Fame in 1946.

04 May

On this date in 1960 . . .

P. K. Wrigley made one of the strangest managerial changes in baseball by calling Lou Boudreau out of the WGN radio booth to manage the Cubs, replacing Charlie Grimm. Wrigley also sent Grimm to replace Boudreau as announcer. At the time of the move, the Cubs had a record of 6-11. Boudreau had previously managed the Indians (1942–1950), Red Sox (1952–1954) and Athletics (1955–1957). He had been a radio announcer for the Cubs since 1958. The club continued to play erratically under Boudreau and landed in seventh place by season's end with a record of 60-94. The finish also ended Boudreau's career as manager. He returned to the broadcast booth in 1961 and remained there until retiring in 1988. During that period, he was elected to baseball's Hall of Fame in 1970.

05 May

On this date in 1883 . . .

The Cubs played their first game at remodeled Lakefront Park. According to Michael Gershman in his book *Diamonds,* the ballpark was the first "marketed as an attraction in its own right" and set new standards for fan comfort. Lakefront Park had the largest seating capacity in baseball, holding 10,000, including 2,000 in the standing room section. A pagoda built as a bandstand overlooked the main entrance and provided more room. Baseball's first "Skyboxes" sat above the stands on the third base side. The 18 plush luxury boxes featured armchairs and curtains to keep out the sun and wind. Team owner Albert Spalding had his own box, which included a telephone, an invention patented only in 1876, "to enable him to conduct the details of the game without leaving his seat" and a Chinese gong to summon employees. The gong later moved to West Side Park and was used to signal the start of the game. A bicycle track surrounded the field to supplant Spalding's income on non-playing days. Forty-one people, including seven ushers, six policemen, four ticket sellers, three field men, three cushion renters, six refreshment boys and eight musicians, staffed Lakefront Park.

06 May

On this date in 1998 . . .

In one of the most dominating pitching performances in Cubs history, Kerry Wood pitched a one-hitter and tied a major league record by striking out 20 batters to shut out the Astros 2-0 at Wrigley Field. Wood surpassed the National League record of 19 previously held by four other pitchers and the major league rookie record of 18. The previous Cubs' high for strikeouts in a game was by Jack Pfeister who fanned 17 in a 15-inning game in 1906. The nine-inning mark was 16 by John Clarkson in 1886. It was only the fourth major league start for Wood, who was 20 years old. The only other pitcher to strike out as many batters at his age was Bob Feller, who fanned 17 as a 17-year-old with the Indians in 1936. Wood opened the game with five straight strikeouts and entered the ninth with six strikeouts in a row and 18 in the game. In the ninth, Wood struck out Billy Spiers swinging on a 1-2 pitch for his seventh strikeout in succession, retired Craig Biggio on a ground out and fanned Derek Bell swinging on a 1-2 count. The only two Houston base runners were Rick Gutierrez on a third-inning single and Biggio who was hit by a pitch in the sixth. Wood threw 122 pitches in the game, 84 of them for strikes.

The question of the day.

Who was Bill Hutchinson?

Hutchinson pitched for the Cubs from 1889 through 1895. Few fans today would recognize the name, but he is among the leaders in several club career statistical lists. Hutchinson is third in wins (182), first in defeats (158), first in complete games (317), first in walks (1,109), second in innings (3,021), third in games started (339), sixth in games pitched (367), sixth in strikeouts (1,222) and 10th in shutouts (21). In 1890, 1891 and 1892, he led the NL in wins, games, games started, complete games and innings. Hutchinson's totals for innings pitched those three seasons were 603, 561 and 622. He accounted for 42 of the Cubs' 84 wins in 1890, 44 of 82 in 1891 and 36 of 70 in 1892. No pitcher since 1892 has accounted for 50 percent of his club's victories. At the time, the pitching distance to home plate was 55 feet. In 1893, it was increased to 60 feet, six inches, and no one pitched more than 500 innings at that distance as the extra five feet put a strain on endurance pitchers like Hutchinson. The last pitcher with at least 400 innings pitched in a season was Ed Walsh of the White Sox in 1908. The last hurler with 300 or more innings was Steve Carlton with the Phillies in 1980.

On this date in 1973 . . .

Ernie Banks became the first African American to manage a team in major league history. Banks was a coach with the Cubs and took over direction of the club following the ejection of manager Whitey Lockman. The Cubs defeated the Padres 3-2 in 12 innings in San Diego. A year later, Reverend Jesse Jackson, national president of Operation PUSH (People United to Save Humanity) accused the Cubs of racism for the failure to hire Banks as manager. Owner P. K. Wrigley responded by stating that Banks was "too nice" to be a manager and that if he wanted the position he would arrange for Banks to serve an apprenticeship in the minors. "All I can say," declared Wrigley, "is that being a major league manager is like being a kamikaze pilot. It's suicide." Frank Robinson became the first permanent African American manager in the majors when hired by the Indians in October 1974. The first to be hired by the Cubs was Don Baylor in November 1999.

The question of the day.

How did the Cubs miss out on signing Joe DiMaggio?

DiMaggio played for the San Francisco Seals in the Pacific Coast League at the age of 19 in 1934, and the Cubs had the first option of purchasing his contract. P. K. Wrigley refused to appropriate the money, however. DiMaggio suffered a knee injury that season getting out of a cab, and Wrigley believed he was a damaged good. The owner of the Seals offered Wrigley a money-back guarantee. The Cubs were allowed to try out DiMaggio during spring training in 1935, and if the club believed he was not a prospect, he could be returned for a full refund of the purchase price. Wrigley still turned down the offer because the Cubs were well fortified in the outfield with players like Chuck Klein, Kiki Cuyler, Augie Galan and Frank Demaree. The Yankees had few qualms about DiMaggio's health and bought him from the Seals for $25,000 and five minor league players on December 19, 1934. After another season in San Francisco, DiMaggio arrived in the majors in 1936 and was an immediate sensation.

On this date in 1876 . . .

The Cubs played their first National League game in Chicago and defeated Cincinnati 6-0 at the 23rd Street Grounds. The Chicago ballpark was built in 1872 shortly after the fire that devastated the city in October of 1871. It was located on a block bounded by the present day streets of West 23rd Street, State Street, West 22nd Street and South Federal Street. The 23rd Street Grounds was a ramshackle facility with a wooden grandstand that could seat perhaps 1,500 fans and had a short wooden fence surrounding the playing field that was only about six or seven feet high. The outfield dimensions are unknown, but at least two balls cleared the right-field barrier at a time when a 300-foot drive was considered to be a mammoth clout. The fences in that era were not conceived as home run targets, but merely as a means of ensuring that fans would have to pay to enter and see the games. The Cubs used the 23rd Street Grounds in 1876 and 1877.

On this date in 1996 . . .

The Mets defeated the Cubs 7-6 at Shea Stadium in a game interrupted by a long and ugly brawl. There were nine ejections, including four Cubs. In the fifth inning with New York leading 6-3, Chicago reliever Terry Adams threw a pitch behind Mets pitcher Pete Harnisch, who then had words with catcher Scott Servais. Harnisch threw a sucker punch at Servais around umpire Greg Bonin, and both benches and bullpens emptied. It took 16 minutes to restore order. The brawl whirled its way around the infield, into foul territory and down the Cubs dugout steps. By the time it was over, hats and gloves were strewn all over the field. Chicago players ejected were Servais, Scott Bullett, Leo Gomez and Turk Wendell.

On this date in 1955 . . .

Sam Jones of the Cubs pitched a no-hitter, defeating the Pirates 4-0 before a crowd of only 2,918 at Wrigley Field. In the ninth inning, Jones walked Gene Freese, Preston Ward and Tom Saffell to load the bases with nobody out. With the tying run at the plate, manager Stan Hack went to the mound to confer with Jones, and after a brief discussion, decided to leave the pitcher in the game. Jones then proceeded to strike out Dick Groat, Roberto Clemente and Frank Thomas on 12 pitches, two of which were two-strike foul balls, to end the game. Jones finished the game with seven walks and six strikeouts. He was the first African American pitcher in major league history to pitch a no-hitter. Nicknamed "Toothpick Sam" because he pitched with a toothpick in his mouth, Jones had a 14-20 record for the Cubs in 1955, walking 185 batters and striking out 198 in 242⅓ innings. The 185 walks is a Cubs record for a season. Jones led the league in walks and strikeouts in both 1955 and 1956, his only two seasons with the Cubs. He was traded to the Cardinals in an eight-player deal on December 11, 1956.

13 May

On this date in 1896 . . .

A riot nearly erupted at West Side Grounds in Chicago over the decisions of umpire Tim Keefe during a game against Boston. Keefe was the lone umpire on the field that day, a practice common in the era. In the 10th inning, with the score tied 4-4, Bill Everett of the Cubs lined a ball down the left-field line that looked good for a triple. With Keefe's attention focused on the ball, Boston first baseman Tommy Tucker grabbed Everett around the neck and threw him to the ground as he rounded the bag. Everett popped up and began to fight with Tucker. During the altercation, second baseman Bobby Lowe retrieved the ball and tagged Everett. Keefe called Everett out, ignoring the obvious interference. At the end of the 10th, with the score still deadlocked, Chicago manager Cap Anson believed it was too dark to continue and appealed to the umpire to stop play. Keefe thought otherwise and ordered the start of the 11th inning. The Cubs did everything they could to prolong the game so that the inning could not be completed. Boston made six runs as the Cubs made one error after another and made no attempts to retire the opposition on the base paths. Keefe finally stopped the game and awarded a forfeit to Boston.

14 May

On this date in 1881 . . .

A "rally hen" and the big dog of Cubs owner William Hulbert helped the club win a 4-3 decision over Worcester in Chicago. Cubs players believed that a black hen found near the ballpark was good luck, and in the seventh inning they let the hen run loose on the field with Worcester leading 3-2. In the ninth, the Cubs scored two runs to win the game. Tom Burns drove in the winning run with a long drive toward the clubhouse, which was in play in left field. Hulbert's dog was sleeping on the clubhouse platform, and Worcester outfielder Buttercup Dickerson was afraid of the animal, or at least pretended to be. The dog paid no attention to Dickerson, but Worcester claimed interference, a "silly protest" that was denied by the umpires. It was Worcester's first loss after an 8-0 start. Six days later when Boston came to town, a discussion about the dog took place prior to the game. The Boston club demanded the removal of the canine from the clubhouse platform and that the clubhouse doors be closed to prevent a ball from being hit through the opening. "There's no rule covering dogs and doors," barked Hulbert. "But if it will make you any happier, the dog shall be bounced and the door closed."

On this date in 1960 . . .

Don Cardwell pitched a no-hitter in his first game as a Chicago Cub, leading his new club to a 4-0 win over the Cardinals before 33,542 fans in the second game of a double-header at Wrigley Field, which followed a 6-1 Cubs defeat in the first contest. Alex Grammas, who reached on a walk with one out in the first inning, was the only St. Louis base runner during Cardwell's gem. Cardwell retired the next 26 batters to face him. In the ninth, Carl Sawatski was retired on a leaping catch by George Altman in front of the right-field wall. George Crowe popped up to Richie Ashburn in center for the second out. Joe Cunningham followed with a hump back liner on a 3-2 pitch to left field. It looked like a certain hit, but Walt Moryn made a miraculous running catch off his shoe tops. Cardwell finished the day with seven strikeouts. He came to the Cubs two days earlier in a trade with the Phillies along with Ed Bouchee for Tony Taylor and Cal Neeman. Cardwell was 24 years old with an undistinguished 17-26 lifetime record when he threw the no-hitter. He was 30-44 in three seasons as a Cub and finished his career in 1970 with a mark of 102-138.

On this date in 2000 . . .

Fans at Wrigley Field became engaged in a melee with Dodgers players in the stands. An individual who hit Los Angeles catcher Chad Krueter in the head, then stole his cap triggered the incident. Krueter entered the stands to try and stop the assailant. Other members of the Dodgers bullpen crew followed Krueter before the rest of the team raced over from the dugout. With beer flying, and fans and players fighting, it took nine minutes to quell the disturbance. Cubs manager Don Baylor and coach Rene Lachemann came over to ask the fans to behave. Four fans were arrested. Suspensions and fines were handed to 16 players, three coaches and the bullpen catcher. Krueter was suspended for eight days and fined $5,000.

On this date in 1979 . . .

The Cubs lost a 23-22 scoring marathon against the Phillies at Wrigley Field. The winning run scored on a two-out, solo homer in the 10th inning by Mike Schmidt off Bruce Sutter. Aided by blustery conditions, the two teams combined for 11 home runs to tie a National League record. Dave Kingman belted three home runs for the Cubs and drove in six runs. One of them cleared an apartment building on Waveland Avenue and struck a house on Kenmore Avenue. There were a total of 50 hits in the game, 26 of them by the Cubs. The first inning set the tone when the Phillies scored seven runs, and the Cubs came back with six in their half, three of them on Kingman's first homer. Starting pitchers Lerch and Dennis Lamp each retired only one batter before being replaced. The game was tied 22-22 after three Cubs runs in the eighth on five singles. The winning pitcher was Rawly Eastwick, who pitched two perfect innings in the ninth and tenth.

On this date in 1967 . . .

The Cubs installed AstroTurf at Wrigley Field. The green turf, covering come 5,000 square feet, was placed on the empty seats in the center-field bleachers to improve the batters' line of sight. It was one of many solutions the club used over the years. During the 1941 season, the Cubs roped off a section of the bleachers because of complaints by hitters that they lost the flight of the ball in the white shirts of the fans who sat in their line of vision. The center-field section was closed from 1941 through 1947 and opened again from 1948 through 1951. It was closed for good on April 20, 1952, with the exception of the 1962 All-Star Game. The seats were painted dark gray to improve the background before being covered by AstroTurf in 1967. The artificial turf was taken out in 1982, and the seats were painted dark green. Juniper bushes were planted in 1997. During the 2006 remodeling, a large luxury suite was built in center field, fronted by dark slanted windows so as not to interfere with the batters' sight lines. They placed four rows of juniper bushes in front of the luxury suites.

Happy Birthday Turk Wendell.

Relief pitcher Steven "Turk" Wendell was born on this date in 1967. One of the most colorful players in Cubs history, Wendell was a bundle of idiosyncrasies. He chewed Brach's black licorice on the mound and brushed his teeth between innings. Wendell also talked to the baseball, drew crosses in the dirt on the mound and leaped sideways over foul lines. Before he threw his first pitch, Turk waved to the center fielder, and would not face the hitter until the outfielder waved back. He insisted that the umpire roll the ball to the mound rather than simply throw it to him. If an umpire threw the ball to him, Wendell was known to let it go past him or to even let it bounce off his chest, then pick it up off the ground. He also wore a necklace made from the teeth of the animals he had hunted and killed. Wendell wore number 13 with the Cubs and later donned number 99 with the Mets, Phillies and Rockies. He pitched for the Cubs from his rookie year in 1993 until 1997 and was in the majors until 2004.

On this date in 2006 . . .

The Cubs-White Sox rivalry became more heated when a fight broke out between the opposing catchers during a 7-0 Sox win at U.S. Cellular Field. In the second inning, A. J. Pierzynski bowled over Michael Barrett just before the ball arrived on a play at the plate. Pierzynski got up, nudged Barrett and slapped the plate emphatically. Barrett responded by punching Pierzynski with a hard right to the left side of the face. Scott Podsednik of the Sox wrestled Barrett to the ground. During the ensuing bench-clearing melee, John Mabry of the Cubs fought Brian Anderson of the White Sox. As Pierzynski went back to the dugout, he raised his hands in the air as the sellout crowd cheered, then began slapping the hands of his teammates. The battle delayed play for 15 minutes. Barrett, Pierzynski, Mabry and Anderson were all ejected. Barrett was suspended for 10 days because of his participation in the incident. As a result of their fight, Barrett and Pierzynski shook hands on the diamond at Wrigley Field on June 29. The next day, Pierzynski hit a three-run home run that capped a two-out rally in the ninth and lifted the Sox to an 8-6 win. The game was delayed for about five minutes after Pierzynski's home run as fans pelted the field with debris.

On this date in 1927 . . .

Charles Lindbergh landed in Paris after his historic flight across the Atlantic, and the Cubs played a contentious double-header against the Dodgers at Ebbets Field. The previous day during a 7-5 Cubs triumph, Brooklyn fans showered umpire Pete McLaughlin with hundreds of bottles. One of them was a bottle of "bootleg" whiskey, a beverage outlawed during Prohibition. During the May 21 twin bill, the umpires were targets once more, as the Cubs won 6-4 and 11-6. In the second tilt, the Cubs scored nine runs in the ninth inning off five Dodger pitchers for the victory. Hack Wilson's bases-loaded triple put Chicago into the lead. At the conclusion of the contest, special police and several Brooklyn players extracted umpire Frank Wilson from a threatening crowd with great difficulty. It had been agreed before hand that the game would be called at 5:45 p.m. to allow the Cubs to catch a train. Wilson interpreted that to mean that no inning could start after 5:45. Dodger manager Wilbert Robinson believed that the contest would end precisely at 5:45. The ninth inning started at 5:40 and took more than a half hour to complete. Robinson protested the Cubs victory to National League President John Heydler, but the protest was denied.

On this date in 1883 . . .

Cubs outfielder Billy Sunday made his major league debut and struck out four times in four at-bats during a 4-3 Cubs win over Buffalo in Chicago. Despite the inauspicious debut, Sunday played for the Cubs until 1887 and in the majors until 1890. After he quit baseball, Sunday became a fiery, world-famous evangelist, spearheading the prohibition movement and attempting to outlaw Sunday baseball. He would often "slide" onto the stage as if sliding into a base. It is estimated that Sunday preached to more than one million people during his lifetime. The peak of his popularity was during the 1910s. Sunday also became a millionaire while preaching across the country. He dined with Presidents Theodore Roosevelt, Woodrow Wilson and counted Herbert Hoover, John D. Rockefeller, Jr. and several Hollywood notables among his friends. Sunday died in 1935.

On this date in 1946 . . .

The Cubs and Dodgers fought each other for the second day in a row at Ebbets Field. The previous day, Lennie Merullo of the Cubs knocked down Dodger second baseman Eddie Stanky while trying to break up a double play in the 10th inning. Stanky wrapped his legs around Merullo's neck in a scissor hold, and both punched each other until the umpires and the players intervened. During the brawl, Cubs pitcher Claude Passeau ripped the jersey off Brooklyn manager Leo Durocher. During batting practice on May 23, Dixie Walker of the Dodgers took exception to some remarks Merullo made to Pee Wee Reese. Walker wrestled Merullo to the ground. Phil Cavarretta came to Merullo's rescue and landed a few blows to Walker's body before a squad of police arrived and separated the players. Walker had one tooth knocked out and another one chipped. Merullo was fined $150 and suspended eight days by National League President Ford Frick. Cavarretta was fined $100. Cubs coach Red Smith was suspended for five days because he tried to prevent police from breaking up the fight. The Cubs lost the game 2-1 in 11 innings.

On this date in 1957 . . .

Cubs right fielder Frank Ernaga homered in his first major league at-bat and tripled in his second appearance during a 5-1 win over the Braves at Wrigley Field. The home run, struck in the second inning, tied the score 1-1. Ernaga's fourth-inning triple drove in the run that broke the tie. Both hits came off future Hall of Famer Warren Spahn, who won the Cy Young Award in 1957. In his first eight big-league at-bats, Ernaga collected five extra base hits with two homers, two triples and a double. His career lasted only 43 at-bats over two seasons, however, with a final batting average of .279.

On this date in 2001 . . .

A Cubs pitcher hurled a one-hitter for the second day in a row. On May 24, Jon Lieber pitched a one-hitter to beat the Reds 3-0 at Wrigley Field. Juan Castro collected the only Cincinnati hit with a single in the sixth inning after Lieber retired the first 16 batters he faced. Lieber threw only 79 pitches and had to wait out a 97-minute rain delay in the fourth inning. It was the first time the Reds had been shut out since 1999, ending a National League record streak of 208 consecutive games scoring at least one run. On May 25, Kerry Wood one-hit the Brewers for a 1-0 victory at Wrigley Field. Wood struck out 14 batters and carried a no-hit bid into the seventh inning before giving up a leadoff single to Mark Loretta. Only nine teams since 1900 have had back-to-back one-hitters. This is the only time the Cubs have accomplished the feat.

On this date in 1957 . . .

Cubs rookie pitcher Dick Drott struck out 15 batters during a 7-5 win over the Braves in the first game of a double-header at Wrigley Field. Hank Aaron struck out three times. Drott fanned 10 batters in the first five innings and was left in the game by manager Bob Scheffing despite weakening at the end. Drott gave up two runs in the eighth and two more in the ninth. He was only 20 years old on the day of his 15-strikeout performance, and he had a 15-11 record with a 3.58 ERA and 170 strikeouts in 229 innings in 1957. He seemed destined for stardom, but the Cubs pushed the youngster far too hard, far too early in his career, and Drott broke down quickly after his fine rookie season. The Cubs gave him up to Houston in the expansion draft following the 1961 season, and Drott's career ended two years later with a record of 27-46. From 1958 through 1963, Drott had a won-lost record of 12-35 with an earned run average of 5.38.

On this date in 1984 . . .

A disputed call by third base umpire Steve Rippley created a ruckus during a Cubs-Reds game at Wrigley Field. In the second inning, Ron Cey struck a Mario Soto pitch down the left-field line, which Rippley called a home run. Furious, Soto rushed toward the umpire and bumped into him. During the course of the argument, the Reds pitcher had to be wrestled to the ground by manager Vern Rapp and catcher Brad Gulden. In the process of restraining Soto, they collided with Cubs third base coach Don Zimmer, prompting both benches to empty. During the ensuing melee, a vendor threw a bag of ice that struck Soto in the chest. The seething Soto grabbed a bat and tried to climb into the stands but was stopped before he could inflict bodily harm. Meanwhile, the umpires conferred and reversed the home run ruling, reducing Cey's drive to a mere foul ball. Cubs manager Jim Frey went berserk over the decision and was ejected along with Soto. In all, the game was delayed for 32 minutes. Play resumed, and the Reds won 4-3.

On this date in 1930 . . .

Cubs pitcher Hal Carlson died suddenly from a stomach hemorrhage at 3:35 a.m. in his apartment at a North Side hotel. He was 36 years old. Carlson arose shortly after 2 a.m. after being unable to sleep because of the pain. He called teammates Riggs Stephenson, Kiki Cuyler and Cliff Heathcote, who summoned the team physician, Dr. John Davis. Carlson died shortly after Davis arrived. He had suffered from stomach ulcers for two years and often predicted he would die suddenly of the illness.

On this date in 1962 . . .

Ernie Banks hit a double and three consecutive home runs, although the Cubs lost 11-9 to the Braves at Wrigley Field. It was Ernie's first game since being hit on the head with a pitch on May 25. He doubled in the second inning, then poled homers off Bob Hendley in the third, Don Nottebart in the fifth and Lew Burdette in the seventh. On the same day, the Cubs hired Buck O'Neill as a coach, and he became the first African American coach in major league history. He remained as a coach until 1965, although he spent little time with the Cubs. O'Neill's duties consisted mainly of serving as an instructor and scout in the club's minor league system. The Cubs had employed him as a scout since 1955. Prior to that, O'Neill was manager of the Kansas City Monarchs of the Negro League. Among his players were Banks, George Altman and Elston Howard.

On this date in 1904 . . .

Cubs first baseman Frank Chance set a major league record when was hit five times by Reds pitchers Jack Harper and Win Kellum during a double-header in Cincinnati. The Cubs lost the first game 7-4 but won the second 5-2. Chance emerged from the ordeal with a cut forehead and a black eye. He was hit three times in the first game and lost consciousness once when the pitch hit him in the head. Throughout his playing days, which took place prior to the use of the batting helmet, Chance paid a high price for crowding the plate. He was hit by pitches 137 times during his 17-year career, never played in more than 140 games in a season and topped 130 only once, but he still refused to back away from the plate. The many blows he incurred caused deafness in one ear, and a stint as an amateur boxer also contributed to head injuries. During a game on July 1, 1911, Chance collapsed on the field because of a blood clot on his brain. Blinding headaches ended his playing career and contributed to his early death at age 46.

31
May

On this date in 2003 . . .

In the longest 1-0 game in Wrigley Field history, the Cubs edged the Astros in a 16-inning marathon. It was a blustery day at the ballpark with temperatures standing at 48 degrees accompanied by 24-mile-per-hour wind gusts. Sammy Sosa drove in the lone run of the day with a single after striking out five times in his previous six appearances. Carlos Zambrano (eight innings), Mike Remlinger (two-thirds of an inning), Antonio Alfonseca (1⅓ innings), Joe Borowski (two innings), Kyle Farnsworth (two innings) and Todd Wellemeyer (two innings) combined on the shutout, allowing just six hits.

Wrigley Hits 100

June

01
June

On this date in 2007 . . .

A fight between Carlos Zambrano and Michael Barrett highlighted an 8-5 loss to the Braves at Wrigley Field. Following a five-run Atlanta fifth inning, Zambrano pointed at his head and yelled at Barrett before shoving him. On a single play during the inning, Barrett was charged with a passed ball and a throwing error. Moments later, the two fought again in the clubhouse, and the catcher emerged with two black eyes and a cut lip that required six stitches and hospitalization. It happened on Zambrano's 26th birthday. The club fined both players an undisclosed amount, and Zambrano publicly apologized for the incident. The Cubs traded Barrett to the Padres 19 days later. The Zambrano-Barrett clash also coincided with a turn of fortune for the 2007 Cubs. The club was 22-31 on June 2 and went 63-48 the rest of the way to win the NL Central title.

02
June

On this date in 1908 . . .

During a heated argument in the clubhouse, Heinie Zimmerman threw a bottle of ammonia at Cubs teammate Jimmy Sheckard before a 12-4 loss to the Pirates at West Side Grounds in Chicago. The bottle hit Sheckard in the forehead and exploded. It was feared that he might be permanently blinded. Fortunately, Cook County Hospital was located across the street from the ballpark, and medical personnel were able to respond quickly, saving his eyesight. Player-manager Frank Chance tore into Zimmerman, and the two were embroiled in a fistfight. Zimmerman held his own against Chance and appeared to be winning the bout when Cubs players jumped in, beating Zimmerman so badly that he too had to carted off to the hospital. Both Sheckard and Zimmerman were out of action for a month. Despite the incident, Sheckard and Zimmerman would share the same clubhouse through the end of the 1912 season, when Sheckard was traded to the Cardinals.

On this date in 2003 . . .

Sammy Sosa was ejected from a 3-2 win over Tampa Bay at Wrigley Field for using cork in his bat. Sosa shattered his bat on a grounder to second, leading to the discovery of the illegal cork. Sosa contended that he used corked bats for home run exhibitions and had inadvertently selected the bat for his first-inning plate appearance. Major league baseball officials suspended him for eight games on June 6, but he appealed the suspension. After a hearing on June 11, the suspension was reduced to seven games. The league tested 76 bats confiscated from Sosa's locker and found no foreign substances. Five of his bats from the Hall of Fame were also examined and found to be clean. At the end of the season, Sosa had 40 homers and a .279 batting average.

On this date in 1981 . . .

The Cubs purchased Bobby Bonds from the Rangers. Bonds was 36 years old and had fallen a long way from his peak during the 1970s, when he was regarded as one of the best players in baseball. The Cubs were his eighth team since 1974. Bonds spent the first two months of the 1981 season with the Rangers' farm team in Wichita, Kansas, and hit .244. He arrived only an hour before the Cubs' June 4 game against the Pirates in Pittsburgh and was placed in the starting lineup hitting clean up, but he never got to bat that day. In the first inning, the Pirates retired the Cubs in order, sending them out to play defense before Bonds could step to the plate. On the fourth pitch of the bottom of the first, he fell trying to catch a short fly to right field by Tim Foli and broke the little finger on his left hand. The Cubs lost 5-4 in 10 innings. A week later, the players went on strike for nearly two months. Bonds would play 45 games with the Cubs but batted only .215 with six home runs.

05 June

On this date in 1962 . . .

Cubs shortstop Andre Rodgers not only blew a chance at a triple play, but also failed to record an out during an 11-4 loss to the Giants at Wrigley Field. With Jim Davenport on second, Tom Haller on first and nobody out, the San Francisco base runners were on the move when Jose Pagan whistled a line drive straight at Rodgers, who dropped the ball as he turned toward second. It would have been an easy triple play if he made the catch, because all he had to do was step on second and tag Haller, who was already moving into the bag. At the end of the play, the Giants had the bases loaded and scored three more runs before the inning ended. Through 2008, there have been only 14 unassisted triple plays in big-league history. Cubs shortstop Jimmy Cooney pulled off one on May 30, 1927, during a 10-inning, 7-6 win over the Pirates in the first game of a double-header in Pittsburgh. The play came in the fourth inning with Lloyd Waner on second and Clyde Barnhart on first. Cooney snagged Paul Waner's liner, stepped on second to double Paul's brother Lloyd and then tagged Barnhart coming down from first.

06 June

On this date in 1885 . . .

The Cubs played their first game at West Side Park and beat St. Louis 9-2 before a crowd of 10,327. It was located on a block bounded by Congress Street, Loomis Street, Harrison Street and Throop Street. It was a lavish ballpark for its day, with the woodwork painted a terra cotta shade. A 12-foot-high brick wall surrounded it. The ballpark had seating for 10,000 and included private rooftop boxes in addition to facilities for track, cycling and lawn tennis. It also offered, according to promotional material, a "neatly furnished toilet room with a private entrance for ladies." Spectators entered the stands by a 16-foot stairway. The playing field was bathtub-shaped, with 216-foot foul lines and a deep center field. Fans arriving by carriage could reach the grandstand through a covered entrance inside the grounds and park their vehicles in deep center field. The carriages were in play, although few balls were hit that far. Occasionally, however, outfielders had to risk life and limb retrieving balls that were hit under the hooves of the horses. Because of the short foul lines, West Side Park was a home run haven. From 1885 through 1890, the Cubs hit 318 home runs at the facility but only 92 while on the road.

On this date in 1906 . . .

The Cubs scored 11 runs in the first inning and annihilated the Giants 19-0 in New York. The Cubs scored the 11 first-inning runs off Christy Mathewson and Joe McGinnity, two of the greatest pitchers of their generation. McGinnity also gave up three runs in the second before he was relieved. Wildfire Schulte collected five of Chicago's 22 hits. At the time, the Cubs and Giants were bitter rivals and accounted for nine of the 10 National League pennants won from 1904 through 1913. For years afterward, Chicago fans taunted Giants fans during games by chanting "Nineteen! Nineteen!" The 1906 contest is one of two since 1900 in which the Cubs scored at least 19 runs in a shutout victory. The other one was on May 13, 1969, over the Padres at Wrigley Field. It was the third consecutive game where the Cubs shut out the opposition, with Dick Selma hurling a complete game. Ernie Banks was the hitting star with seven runs batted in on two homers and a double. The all-time record for most runs in a shutout win by a Chicago team was a 20-0 rout of Washington in the Nation's Capital on May 28, 1886.

The question of the day.

Who was Andrew Brennan?

Andrew Brennan built rooftop seats on his Taylor Street residence in 1899 that overlooked the West Side Grounds, the Cubs' home field from 1893 through 1915. The Cubs protested and with the help of police, tried to stop Brennan. A Chicago judge issued an injunction restraining the ball club, the city and James McAndrews of the Department of Public Works from interfering with Brennan, who was free to rent the seats on his rooftop building to those who wished to watch Cubs games. Taylor Street was located behind the right-field wall, and Brennan's home was directly across the street from West Side Grounds. Brennan found plenty of imitators among his neighbors, who also built rooftop bleachers. The practice stopped in 1908 when a fan named William Hudson fell from one of the roofs to his death. Hudson dropped from the perch four stories above the pavement in the excitement over Joe Tinker's home run off Christy Mathewson that beat the Giants 1-0 on July 17. The next day, the city condemned many of the structures, which held as many as 1,000 fans, as unsafe. In 1909, the Cubs built a 61-foot-high wall behind the right-field bleachers that blocked the view from the Taylor Street rooftops. A few years later, the wall reached a height of 80 feet.

09 June

The question of the day.

Who holds the Cubs record for most runs batted in during a game?

Heinie Zimmerman and Sammy Sosa are the co-holders of the record with nine. Zimmerman established the mark as the Cubs walloped the Boston Braves 20-2 in Chicago. Zimmerman drove in the nine runs on a pair of three-run homers and two singles. Jimmy Sheckard scored five times, to tie another modern (since 1900) club record. Sosa drove in nine with three consecutive three-run homers in three consecutive innings during a 15-1 rout of the Rockies in Denver. Sammy left the game in the sixth inning before having a chance at a major league-record fourth home run. He went deep on Shawn Chacon in the third and fourth innings and on Mark Corey in the fifth. Sosa was only the fifth player in big-league history to hit a home run in three consecutive innings. It was also the sixth time that Sosa hit at least three homers in a game, tying the record set by Johnny Mize between 1938 and 1950 while with the Cardinals, Giants and Yankees. Sosa also hit three home runs in a single contest on June 5, 1996; June 15, 1998; August 9, 2001; August 22, 2001; and September 23, 2001.

10 June

On this date in 1912 . . .

Heinie Zimmerman hit a game-winning homer in the 10th inning, on what was supposed to be an intentional walk, to lift the Cubs to a 9-8 win over the Giants in New York. With the score tied 7-7 and Joe Tinker on third, Giants manager John McGraw ordered pitcher Doc Crandall to intentionally walk Zimmerman. Heinie had other plans, however, and took a running jump, swatting the ball high over his head and driving it into the right-field stands. Earlier in the game, Zimmerman went long into the left-field bleachers.

On this date in 1904 . . .

In a sensational pitching performance, Bob Wicker of the Cubs pitched 12 innings and allowed only one hit in defeating the Giants 1-0 before 38,805 spectators in New York, the largest crowd in major league history up to that point. Wicker held the Giants hitless through the first nine innings and was deprived of a no-hitter when his teammates failed to score against Joe McGinnity, who entered the contest with a 14-game winning streak. The only New York hit was an infield single by Sam Mertes with one out in the 10th inning that deflected off the hands of Chicago third baseman Doc Casey. Wicker struck out 10 batters and walked only one. The lone run of the game scored when Frank Chance singled, advanced to third on two infield outs and crossed the plate on a single by Johnny Evers. In appreciation of Wicker's achievement, part of the Polo Grounds crowd carried him off the field on its shoulders.

On this date in 1986 . . .

The Cubs general manager Dallas Green fired Jim Frey as manager along with third base coach Don Zimmer. This set off a bizarre sequence of hirings and firings over a period of 17 months that could only happen with the Cubs. Gene Michael replaced Frey as manager. Then, WGN radio hired Frey as an announcer for Cubs games. On September 8, 1987, Michael resigned as manager, and Frank Lucchesi replaced him on an interim basis. On October 29, 1987, Green resigned as general manager. Two weeks later on November 13, Frey was hired as general manager to replace Green. And on November 20, Frey hired Zimmer as manager. The two went way back. Frey and Zimmer were teammates on the baseball team at Western Hills High School in Cincinnati.

13
June

On this date in 1984 . . .

The Cubs traded Joe Carter, Mel Hall, Don Schulze and Darryl Banks to the Indians for Rick Sutcliffe, George Frazier and Ron Hassey. At the time of the trade, the Cubs had a record of 34-25, and general manager Dallas Green believed it was time to make a trade to help the Cubs win in 1984. He sacrificed four promising youngsters under the age of 25 for three veterans. Sutcliffe was phenomenal over the remainder of the 1984 season. Utilizing a herky-jerky delivery that kept hitters off stride, he was 16-1 with an ERA of 2.69. Sutcliffe won the National League Cy Young Award. Without the trade, it is unlikely the Cubs would have won the division title in 1984, but it hurt the club in the long term. Carter was a five-time All-Star, and Hall became a productive starter for several clubs. Sutcliffe pitched inconsistently for the Cubs after his Cy Young season and was 66-64 with the Cubs from 1985 through 1991.

14
June

On this date in 1986 . . .

Gene Michael was ejected from his first game as manager of the Cubs, a 1-0 loss to the Cardinals at Wrigley Field. Prior to the contest, umpire Eric Gregg warned both managers about pitchers throwing at batters. When a Scott Sanderson pitch in the seventh inning sent Terry Pendleton into the dirt, Gregg booted the Cubs pitcher, and according to the rules, that meant an ejection for the manager as well. Michael managed the Cubs to a 112-122 record before resigning on September 8, 1987. He was too laid back to suit the intense Dallas Green, but he did not go quietly. "I have no respect for Dallas Green," Michael said. "He isn't very sharp and is always covering up for his mistakes. He's a big buffoon with a big mouth. He didn't make a mistake in hiring me. His mistake was not listening to me." Green also resigned seven weeks later.

15 *June*

On this date in 1964 . . .

The Cubs dealt Lou Brock, Paul Toth and Jack Spring to the Cardinals for Ernie Broglio, Bobby Shantz and Doug Clemens. The transaction still rankles Cub fans, even those who were not yet born in 1964. Brock went on to a Hall of Fame career and played in three World Series for the Cards. In three seasons as a Cub, Broglio had a 7-19 record and an ERA of 5.40. At the time, most Cubs fans believed their club got the better of the deal; most St. Louis fans were outraged. The Cubs were 27-27 and only five games out of first place. General manager John Holland believed a bold move was needed to put the club over the hump. The biggest need was a fourth dependable starting pitcher behind Dick Ellsworth, Larry Jackson and Bob Buhl. Brock was viewed as a player who could do little but steal a base. Three days shy of his 25th birthday, he had a career batting average of .257 with just 20 homers in 1,207 at-bats and was a liability on defense. Broglio, 28, had a record of 18-8 and a 2.99 ERA in 1963. He was off to a rough start in 1964, but Holland believed Broglio would return to his winning ways. Within weeks, however, it was apparent to both the fans and Cubs management alike that they made a horrible mistake.

16 *June*

On this date in 2007 . . .

Carlos Zambrano lost a no-hitter in the eighth inning, and the game in the ninth, as the Cubs dropped a 1-0 decision to the Padres at Wrigley Field. Tempers flared in the tight game, and in the fourth inning, the teams erupted in a bench-clearing brawl. It started when Padres hurler Chris Young hit Derrek Lee with a pitch. Lee yelled at Young on the way to first base. Young walked toward Lee, who responded with a punch. Young fought back, and both benches joined in the fray. Young and Lee were both ejected, along with Cubs hitting coach Gerald Perry. Zambrano held the Padres hitless for 7⅓ innings before Marcus Giles reached base on an infield single. Russell Branyan homered in the ninth for the lone run of the game. Those were the only two hits Zambrano allowed.

17
June

On this date in 1962 . . .

Lou Brock hit a home run into the center-field bleachers at the Polo Grounds in New York during an 8-7 win over the Mets. Brock drilled a pitch by Al Jackson approximately 470 feet. The bleachers were constructed in 1923 and were more than 450 feet from home plate. The Polo Grounds was the home of the Giants from 1911 through 1957, and the Mets in 1962 and 1963. Prior to Brock, the only player to homer into the bleachers was Joe Adcock of the Braves in 1953. Oddly, Hank Aaron hit another home run into the bleachers the next day. No one else reached the seats before the ballpark closed at the end of the 1963 season.

18
June

On this date in 1904 . . .

A fan riot nearly erupted in Cincinnati when hundreds of spectators surrounded umpire Gus Moran after the Cubs defeated the Reds 4-1. The fans were angered at a sixth-inning call that went against the Reds, and they swarmed the field, harassing Moran as he made his way to the dressing room. Park police eventually dispersed the crowd but not before someone threw a rock through the window of the dressing room. Fortunately, Moran was not injured. On July 26, Moran encountered more trouble at a Cubs-Reds game, this time in Chicago, as fans reacted violently to his calls against the home team. Fans began throwing bottles onto the field, and the base lines were soon covered with splintered glass. Several hundred fans waited for Moran after the game, and police smuggled the umpire out of the ballpark through a rear gate into a waiting cab.

On this date in 1953 . . .

A controversial grand slam by Cubs third baseman Randy Jackson in the fifth inning off Billy Loes of the Dodgers put the Cubs ahead 8-6 at Wrigley Field. The Cubs went on to win 11-8 in the first game of a double-header, played on a day in which the temperature in Chicago reached 102 degrees. The Dodgers protested Jackson's slam, claiming the drive struck the screen in front of the catwalk in the left-field bleachers. The umpires said the ball cleared the screen and was touched by a fan, causing it to bounce back onto the field. Pee Wee Reese and Duke Snider were ejected during the argument. Brooklyn won the second game 7-1. The next day, the two clubs played in 104-degree heat, the highest temperature ever recorded in Chicago, and the Cubs lost 5-3 at Wrigley Field. Jackson was the Cubs' starting third baseman from 1951 through 1955 and played in two All-Star Games. His given name was Ransom, and he resembled actor Gregory Peck earning Jackson the nickname "Handsome Ransom." Jackson was also a football star as a halfback at the University of Texas.

The question of the day.

When did the Cubs begin wearing uniform numbers?

The National League was established in 1876, but players did not begin wearing uniform numbers on a permanent basis until the 1932 season when the organization passed an edict requiring its clubs to attach the numerals to the backs of the jerseys. The 1929 Yankees were the first team to permanently use uniform numbers. The first Cubs numbers were issued to Woody English (1), Billy Herman (2), Kiki Cuyler (3), Riggs Stephenson (4), Johnny Moore (5), Charlie Grimm (6), Gabby Hartnett (7), Rollie Hemsley (8), Rogers Hornsby (9), Billy Jurges (11), Charley Root (12), Guy Bush (14), Pat Malone (15), Burleigh Grimes (16), Lon Warneke (17), Bob Smith (18), Jakie May (19), Bud Tinning (21), Marv Gudat (22), LeRoy Herrmann (23), Stan Hack (31), Zack Taylor (34), coach Red Corriden (41), coach Charley O'Leary (49), Frank Demaree (51) and Lance Richbourg (56). Numbers 1 through 7 corresponded to the batting order used by the Cubs at the time. The number-eight hitter, Billy Jurges, was given number 11. For reasons unknown, the Cubs did not issue any numbers ending in zero until 1937.

21
June

On this date in 1928 . . .

Hack Wilson fought a fan during a double-header against the Cardinals at Wrigley Field. The Cubs won the first game 2-1 but lost the second 4-1. After grounding out in the bottom of the ninth in the second game, Wilson climbed into the stands and attacked Edward Young, a milkman who had spent the afternoon hurling insults at the Cubs center fielder. Some 5,000 people swarmed the field before police and the players, led by Gabby Hartnett and Joe Kelly, succeeded in parting Wilson and Young. After the field was cleared, Riggs Stephenson popped up for the final out. National League President John Heydler fined Wilson $100 and Judge Francis P. Allgretti fined Young $1. It was not the first time that Wilson was in trouble with law enforcement, however. On May 23, 1926, police arrested Hack and several companions at a friend's apartment, for drinking beer in violation of the Prohibition Act. At 11 p.m., four Chicago police officers arrived to put a stop to the illegal drinking. Hack tried to slip out the side door but was nabbed. Wilson was fined just $1 in court for the infraction.

22
June

The question of the day.

What batter had two three-home run games against the same pitcher?

Hank Sauer had two games during his 15-year career in which he hit three home runs in a game, and both were accomplished against Curt Simmons of the Phillies. On August 28, 1950, Sauer walloped three consecutive home runs off Simmons in the second, fourth and sixth innings to lead the Cubs to a 7-5 win in the first game of a double-header at Wrigley Field. Philadelphia won the second tilt 9-5. In seven consecutive games from August 24 through August 28, including two double-headers, Sauer had 14 hits, including seven home runs and five doubles, in 27 at-bats. On June 11, 1952, Sauer hit three more homers off Simmons to account for all of the Chicago runs in a 3-2 win over the Phillies at Wrigley Field. Sauer clouted homers in the second, sixth and eighth innings. Despite his heroics, the Cubs would have lost if it were not for a base running blunder by Tommy Brown of the Phillies. With the game tied 1-1 in the fourth inning and two out, Richie Ashburn hit a bases-loaded single that scored two runs and sent Brown from first to third. Brown failed to touch second base, however, negating the two runs. In an inexplicable transaction, the Cubs purchased Brown from the Phillies four days later.

23 June

On this date in 1984 . . .

One of the most dramatic and unforgettable victories in the history of the Cubs took place. Ryne Sandberg hit two home runs and three singles, driving in seven runs to spark the Cubs to a thrilling 11-inning, 12-11 win over the Cardinals in a nationally televised game at Wrigley Field. St. Louis took a 7-1 lead in the second and was up 9-3 in the sixth when the Cubs scored five runs, the last two on a Sandberg single. It was still 9-8 when Sandberg faced Bruce Sutter with two out in the ninth. Ryne hit a home run to tie the game 9-9. The Cards scored twice in the 10th, and in the bottom of the inning, Sandberg brought the crowd to their feet again with a two-out, two-run homer to tie the score 11-11. The Cubs finally won in the 11th when Leon Durham singled, reached third on a stolen base and an error and scored on a pinch-hit single by Dave Owen. The Cubs entered the game with a 36-31 record and had lost six of their previous eight games. From that point to the end of the regular season, the Cubs were 60-34. In his third full season in the majors, Sandberg blossomed into a star, winning the NL MVP Award.

24 June

The question of the day.

Why did Johnny Evers miss most of the 1911 season?

Evers suffered a nervous breakdown on May 5, 1911, after a series of personal tragedies during the previous eight months. He missed the 1910 World Series with a broken leg, and the limb was slow in healing. Then, he caught pneumonia. In December 1910, Evers lost his life savings when his business partner invested in two shoe stores that went bankrupt. Misfortune struck again shortly after the 1911 season started when Evers was the driver in an auto accident that killed his best friend. Tightly wound and temperamental under the best of circumstances, he could not stand the strain. With the exception of one inning in June, Evers did not play again until September. He bounced back in 1912, however, with the best seasons of his career, batting .341 and leading the National League in on-base percentage with a figure of .431. Evers was named player-manager of the Cubs in 1913. No accurate count has been made as to how many times he was ejected by umpires during that season, but he was probably given the thumb in around 20 games.

25
June

On this date in 1970 . . .

The Cubs purchased Milt Pappas from the Braves. Picked up off the waiver wire, Pappas proved to be an excellent acquisition. He found a new home in Chicago and revived his career. Milt won 10 games for the Cubs over the remainder of the 1970 season, and he won 17 more in both 1971 and 1972. He put together one of the greatest pitching performances in Cubs history on September 2, 1971, by retiring the first 26 batters to face him and pitching a no-hitter to defeat the Padres 8-0 before 11,144 fans at Wrigley Field. In the ninth, John Jeter hit a fly ball to Billy Williams in left field, and Fred Kendall grounded out to Don Kessinger at short. Pappas was one out from the first perfect game in Cubs history. He went to a 1-2 count with the next batter, Larry Stahl, but ultimately walked him. Garry Jestadt stepped up to the plate, but Pappas preserved his no-hitter, getting Jestadt to pop out to second baseman Carmen Fanzone. Milt struck out six and threw 98 pitches. There was not another no-hitter by a Cubs pitcher until Carlos Zambrano threw one on September 14, 2008.

26
June

On this date in 1879 . . .

Player-manager Cap Anson was arrested when the Cubs stopped for an exhibition game in Indianapolis. Cubs players Silver Flint and Orator Shafer, who both played baseball in Indianapolis in 1878, left the city with unpaid bills. A constable tried to arrest Flint and Shafer at the ballpark because of the debts, but Anson talked him out of it, explaining that a large crowd had assembled to see the pair play ball and that the arrest might cause a riot. The constable went to the hotel where the Cubs were staying to nab Flint and Shafer after the contest, but the two players escaped in a carriage that took them beyond the city limits. Anson became engaged in a heated argument with the constable at the hotel, and the Cubs skipper wound up being taken to jail for profanity and resisting arrest. Anson was fined $16 by an Indianapolis judge.

On this date in 1997 . . .

The Cubs signed Sammy Sosa to a four-year deal worth $42.5 million, making him the third-highest paid player in baseball behind Barry Bonds and Albert Belle. The deal was heavily criticized at the time. In 1997, Sosa was hardly the third-best player in baseball. Although he hit 36 home runs and had 119 RBIs that season, Sosa batted .251 (the league average was .262) with an on-base percentage of .300 (well below the NL average of .333). He struck out 174 times while drawing only 45 walks. At the end of the 1997 season, Sosa had a career batting average of .257 and an on-base percentage of .308. He was 28 years old, and few players dramatically improve after that age. The contract proved to be a tremendous bargain, however. Becoming more patient and selective at the plate, Sosa hit 66 home runs and drove in 158 runs in 1998 to win the MVP award. His batting average improved to .308, and his on-base percentage rose to .377. From 1998 through 2001, Sosa clobbered 243 home runs, more than any player in major league history over a four-year period, while batting .310 with an on-base percentage of .395.

On this date in 2000 . . .

Pittsburgh ball boy Kierre Bulls helped the Cubs beat the Pirates 5-4 at Three Rivers Stadium. In the fourth inning, Bulls lunged from his chair along the right-field line to cut off a hard-hit double by Joe Girardi that Bulls thought was foul. Umpire Tim McKean, however, had called the ball fair, and the two-base hit scored Damon Buford from first base. McKean did not see the ball deflect off the ball boy's glove and allowed the run to score. McKean should have ruled interference and returned Buford to third base. A similar incident happened at Wrigley Field on September 3, 1936, when Chicago policeman Harry Hanson contributed to a 1-0 loss to the Dodgers in 10 innings. In the first inning, Phil Cavarretta sent a drive down the right-field line. Hanson, stationed on a bench in the Brooklyn bullpen, believed the ball was foul and tossed it to Dodger right fielder Randy Moore. The umpire called interference and sent Cavarretta back to first base. It the ball had gone unimpeded, Cavarretta would have had a double and possibly a triple.

29 June

On this date in 1952 . . .

In one of the most incredible rallies in club history, the Cubs scored seven runs in the ninth inning to defeat the Reds 9-8 in the first game of a double-header in Cincinnati. The rally started with two out and no one on base. The first run scored on a double by Bill Serena, a walk to Roy Smalley and a pinch-hit single from Gene Hermanski. Eddie Miksis reached on an error to score Smalley. Hal Jeffcoat walked to load the bases, and Dee Fondy singled in two runs to make the score 8-5. Hank Sauer doubled in Jeffcoat and Fondy to pull the Cubs within a run. After Bruce Edwards walked, pinch-hitter Johnny Pramesa hit a single to drive in the tying and winning runs. The Cubs lost the second game 9-1.

30 June

On this date in 1959 . . .

Two balls were in play at the same time at Wrigley Field. With St. Louis batting in the fourth inning and the count 3-1 on Stan Musial, Bob Anderson's pitch sailed past catcher Sammy Taylor, walking Musial. Taylor claimed Musial had tipped the pitch and failed to pursue the ball. While Taylor argued with the umpire, Musial went past first and headed for second. Third baseman Al Dark realized the ball was in play and ran to the backstop where the ball was located. With Dark charging in, the batboy tossed the ball to field announcer Pat Pieper, who dropped it to the ground. Dark reached down, grabbed the ball and threw it to shortstop Ernie Banks. Meanwhile, Delmore gave Taylor a new ball as the two continued to argue. Anderson grabbed the ball out of Taylor's hand and threw it to second base at almost the precise moment Dark's throw was headed in the same direction. Anderson's throw sailed into center field, and Musial headed for third. Banks caught Dark's throw and tagged out Musial. The umpires huddled for 10 minutes and ruled that Musial should return to first base. Cubs manager Bob Scheffing protested, and the umps conferred again, this time calling Musial out. Cards skipper Solly Hemus announced his intention to file a formal protest with the league office, but his club won the game 4-1.

Wrigley Hits 100

July

01
July

On this date in 1958 . . .

Entering the game with only one major league homer, Cubs second baseman Tony Taylor hit two during a 9-5 win over the Giants at Wrigley Field. One of Taylor's home runs cleared the wall, while the other was an "inside-the-gutter" homer earned with the ingenious help of his teammates. Leading off the first inning against Johnny Antonelli, Taylor hit a ball just inside the third base line that bounced into the Cubs bullpen and then into a rain gutter at the base of the left-field stands. Cubs players leaped off the bullpen bench as Giant left fielder Leon Wagner came charging over. As the Cubs peered under the bench, Wagner scrambled around looking for the ball, which was actually about 40 feet away, farther down the line in the in the gutter. By the time Wagner realized he had been duped, Taylor had circled the bases. He struck his other home run in the fourth inning facing Ramon Monzant. Taylor did not hit more than one home run in a game again until 1970.

02
July

On this date in 1975 . . .

Cubs outfielder Jose Cardenal was hauled off to jail because of an altercation at O'Hare International Airport. Cardenal's wife Patricia went to the airport to pick him up following a road trip, and she was warned that her car was illegally parked and told to move it. Patricia refused, and by the time her husband had arrived, she was in a fierce argument with Patrol Officer Dennis Dickson. According to Dickson, Jose took the officer's nightstick and clubbed him on the head. Cardenal was taken to the Jefferson Park police station and charged with simple battery, resisting arrest and assaulting a police officer. Cardenal alleged he was the victim of police brutality. The charges against Jose were later dropped, and his wife was fined $250. In August 1976, Cardenal filed a $750,000 suit against the Chicago Police Superintendent James M. Rochford and Officer Dickson. The suit charged Dickson with "physically and verbally" abusing Cardenal and his wife. They settled the case out of court.

The question of the day.

How many Cubs have hit home runs in the All-Star Game?

Seven Cubs have hit home runs in the All-Star Game. They are:
1. Augie Galan (off Schoolboy Rowe in 1936)
2. Hank Sauer (off Bob Lemon in 1952)
3. Ernie Banks (off Bill Monbouquette in 1960)
4. George Altman (off Mike Fornieles in 1961)
5. Billy Williams (off John Wyatt in 1964)
6. Andre Dawson (off Roger Clemens in 1991)
7. Alfonso Soriano (off J. J. Putz in 2007)

On this date in 1895 . . .

More than 35,000 fans watched a separate-admission double-header against the Reds at West Side Grounds in Chicago. In the first game, the crowd was 13,020. The Cubs trailed 7-1 before scoring three runs in the eighth inning, three in the ninth and one in the 10th to win 8-7. Bill Everett's single, his fifth hit of the contest, drove in the winning run. The second game drew 22,913, which taxed the seating capacity of the ballpark. The crush of fans surrounding the diamond shortened the outfield by 100 feet. The crowd delayed the game several times by surging onto the field. The 18 police officers on hand were powerless to stop them. A reserve force of 80 officers marched into the ballpark to great cheers and secured the peace, allowing play to continue. Balls hit into the crowd were homers, and there were 10 of them in the game, six by the Cubs, even though the contest was called because of darkness after seven innings. Walt Wilmot hit two homers for Chicago, and Tim Donahue, Cap Anson, Bill Lange and Everett added one each. Cincinnati pitcher Frank Foreman allowed all six home runs and hit two of his own. The final score was 9-5 in favor of the Cubs.

The question of the day.

Why were the Cubs in the Eastern Division from 1968 through 1993?

In July 1968, the National League voted to divide into two divisions beginning in 1969 because of expansion from 10 teams to 12 with the addition of franchises in Montreal and San Diego. The Cubs were placed in the Eastern Division with Montreal, New York, Philadelphia, Pittsburgh and St. Louis. The Western Division consisted of Atlanta, Cincinnati, Houston, Los Angeles, San Diego and San Francisco. The set up defied geographic logic because Atlanta and Cincinnati are east of Chicago and St. Louis. The Cubs were inserted into the East because of Mets Chairman of the Board M. Donald Grant. In 1968, the three biggest road draws in the National League were the Dodgers, Giants and Cardinals. Grant insisted the Mets be placed in the Eastern Division with at least one of them. St. Louis moved to the East, but agreed only if the Cubs were included. Commissioner Fay Vincent ordered the Cubs and Cardinals to move to the Western Division for the 1993 season, with the Reds and Braves moving east. The Cubs sued to prevent the move. After Vincent resigned in September 1992, the NL scrapped the realignment. Beginning in 1994, the American and National Leagues split into three divisions, with the Cubs joining the NL Central.

On this date in 1913 . . .

After winning the first game of a double-header against the Cardinals 6-0 in Chicago, the Cubs lost the second tilt by forfeit. By prior agreement, game two was to end at 5 p.m. to allow both teams to catch a train. Five innings had to be played to make it an official game. After St. Louis took a 3-0 lead in the third, the club began to make outs deliberately in order to keep the game moving so that five innings would be played on time. The Cubs, on the other hand, stalled to take as much time as possible. The last straw for umpire Mal Eason was a play in which Cardinals catcher Ivy Wingo bunted to Ed Reulbach, who threw the ball wildly to first base. Player-manager Johnny Evers retrieved it but made no attempt to retire Wingo, who slowly trotted around the bases. Eason declared the game a forfeit in favor of the Cards. Evers punched Eason, but somehow escaped a suspension from the National League office.

On this date in 1987 . . .

During a fight-marred 7-5 win over the Padres at Wrigley Field, Padres pitcher Eric Show seemed to purposely hit Cubs slugger Andre Dawson with a pitch, sparking a bench-emptying scuffle. The previous day, Dawson hit two homers out of the park during a 7-0 win over the Padres and added another off Show in the first inning of the July 7 contest. After Show hit Dawson during his next plate appearance in the third inning, Rick Sutcliffe ran out of the dugout toward Show, and both benches emptied. Dawson remained face down for a couple of minutes. When he recovered, he too went after Show, and another fight broke out. Five Cubs players, including Sutcliffe and Dawson, manager Gene Michael and coach Johnny Oates were ejected. Cubs pitcher Scott Sanderson was ejected in the eighth for throwing a pitch behind the head of Chris Brown. Show was not ejected but had to leave the game because he hurt his foot during the brawl. Dawson suffered a lacerated lip and contusions of the cheekbone. He needed 24 stitches to close his wounds.

On this date in 1907 . . .

Player-manager Frank Chance barely escaped bodily harm from the crowd during a 5-0 win over the Dodgers in Brooklyn. Despite the lead, Chance spent much of the game arguing with the umpires, which agitated the throng at the ballpark. As soon as the Cubs took the field in the ninth inning, some of the fans began throwing soda bottles at Chance. After ignoring the first few volleys, he soon became angry, picked up three of the bottles and hurled them into the stands. One of these struck a child, and in an instant, a shower of bottles descended upon Chance. Some of the fans jumped onto the field. Chance stopped to collect more bottles to throw, when Joe Tinker seized him by the arms from behind while the other Cubs checked the advance of the mob. A police escort led Chance from the field. After the game, he had to remain inside the clubhouse for three hours until police could disperse the angry mob waiting outside. Chance left in an armored police car with three officers. National League President Harry Pulliam suspended him for seven days.

09
July

On this date in 1969 . . .

Tom Seaver of the Mets retired the first 25 Cubs batters he faced, but his hopes for a perfect game were wrecked when rookie center fielder Jimmy Qualls singled with one out in the ninth inning. Seaver had to settle for a one-hit, 4-0 win before 59,083 at Shea Stadium. The single that ruined Seaver's gem came in Qualls's 43rd major league at-bat. He played only three years in the majors and ended his big-league career with 63 games played, 31 hits and a .223 batting average. Another obscure Cubs rookie outfielder spoiled a no-hit bid by Seaver on September 24, 1975, when Joe Wallis singled in the ninth inning of an 11-inning, 1-0 victory over the Mets at Wrigley Field. Seaver faced Wallis with two out in the ninth and a no-hitter intact when Wallis rapped a 0-2 pitch into right field for a single. It was only the 15th game of Wallis's career and his 16th hit. The game went into extra innings with the score 0-0. Seaver gave up two more hits in the 10th and exited the game in the top of the 11th for a pinch-hitter. The Cubs won the contest in the bottom of the inning when Mets reliever Skip Lockwood loaded the bases, then walked Bill Madlock. Rick Reuschel (10 innings) and Ken Crosby (one inning) combined on the shutout.

10
July

On this date in 1947 . . .

Left fielder Peanuts Lowrey was pelted with debris during a 10-inning, 4-3 loss to the Dodgers in Brooklyn. When a home run by Carl Furillo bounced out of the left-field bleachers at Ebbets Field, Lowrey tossed it to a fan that then fired it back at Lowrey. The Cubs outfielder angrily threw the ball into the Cubs dugout, bringing a cascade of boos and debris from the crowd. When not getting attacked by fans on the baseball diamond, Lowrey played bit parts in several movies. As a youngster, he appeared in the *Our Gang* comedy serials. As an adult, Lowrey was in baseball movies *Pride of the Yankees* (1942), *The Stratton Story* (1949) and *The Winning Team* (1952). Lowrey's scene in *The Winning Team* called for him to hit Ronald Reagan, playing Grover Alexander, in the head with a baseball. Lowrey's nickname stemmed his grandfather's description of him as an infant as "no bigger than a peanut." His given name was Harry Lee.

11
July

On this date in 2006 . . .

Carlos Zambrano was scheduled to pitch two innings in the All-Star Game at PNC Park in Pittsburgh but was unable to participate after being injured in a freak accident prior to the National League's 3-2 loss. A fungo bat swung by White Sox coach Joey Cora struck Zambrano on the right elbow. Fortunately, the Cubs pitcher was not seriously hurt.

12
July

On this date in 1931 . . .

During a double-header in St. Louis, the Cubs and the Cardinals combined for a record 32 doubles, 23 of them in the second game. The twin bill attracted a record crowd of 45,715 to Sportsman's Park, many of them encircling the outfield. The start of the first game was delayed, and the Cubs could not take infield practice because the fans stole the balls. At game time, fans were wandering around the field, overwhelming the ushers and law enforcement officers. When the police were successful in pushing the crowd back in one sector, it would surge forward in another. Appeals by the umpires were unsuccessful. Police and fire officials were needed to put the excess of 8,000 fans along the outfield walls. The game started with spectators in fair territory only about 70 feet beyond first base, about 100 feet behind third and not more than 150 feet behind second. Balls hit into the overflow were ground rule doubles, which contributed mightily to the record number of two-baggers, many of them mere pop-ups. The throng turned the game into a farce. Outfielders practically played on the heels of the infielders. The Cubs won the first game 7-5, with nine doubles in the contest, five by Chicago batters.

13
July

On this date in 1887 . . .

Cap Anson stopped at third base on a ball hit over the left-field wall during a 3-0 loss to the Senators at Swampoodle Grounds in Washington. Anson hit the ball over the fence with one out in the ninth inning. Left fielder Cliff Carroll pretended he had the ball, and Anson, who was not sure where his drive landed, stopped at second. Anson made a move toward third base, but Carroll made a feint throw, and the Cubs manager-first baseman retraced his steps. This was repeated several times to the vast amusement of the crowd. Anson's teammates convinced him that the ball traveled over the wall, but for some reason, he finally stopped at third base and refused to go any farther.

14
July

On this date in 1920 . . .

Fans witnessed an eventful day at the ballpark as the Cubs lost 3-2 and 4-1 to the Dodgers in Chicago. In the sixth inning of the first game, Ivy Olson of the Dodgers hit a dribbler down the third base line that hopped into the stands and was ruled a home run by umpire Bill Klem. At the time, any ball that reached the stands at least 235 feet from home plate was a home run. The Cubs maintained the ball landed in the box seats less than 235 feet from home, entitling Olson to just two bases. Klem asked for a tape measure, which showed the ball reached the grandstand 241 feet from the plate. Between games, Cubs pitcher Lefty Tyler put on his street clothes and went after a rooter that had been taunting him through the first game. The offensive person was stationed directly in back of the Brooklyn bench, and Tyler gave him an invitation to step outside the ballpark so he could rearrange his face. Club secretary John Seys cooled Tyler off, and two policemen escorted the fan to the elevated station. To add to the general excitement, a visitor from Watertown, Wisconsin, lost his young son, and the park was in turmoil until the lad was found.

The question of the day.

How many times have the Cubs scored at least 30 runs in a game?

There have been only seven instances in which a major league team scored at least 30 runs in a game, and the Cubs have accounted for four them, all in the 19th century. The first was on July 22, 1876, with a 30-7 rout of Louisville in Chicago. The Cubs scored 10 runs in the first inning, eight in the fourth and collected 31 hits in the contest. The Cubs pummeled Cleveland 35-4 in Chicago on July 24, 1882. Dave Rowe pitched the complete game for the Cleveland club. The 35 runs he allowed is the most ever by a major league pitcher in a single game, a record that will likely stand the test of time. Injuries to Jim McCormick and George Bradley, Cleveland's two regular hurlers, pressed Rowe, normally an outfielder, into emergency service. The 31-run victory margin by the Cubs is also the major league record. The Cubs walloped Buffalo 31-7 in Chicago on July 3, 1883. As a team, the Cubs collected a major league record 14 doubles. Buffalo pitcher George Derby pitched the complete game, allowing all 31 runs and 32 hits. The Cubs set a major league record for runs in a game in a 36-7 annihilation of Louisville in Chicago on June 29, 1897.

The question of the day.

Who was Jimmy Archer?

Jimmy Archer played in the majors from 1904 through 1918 and was with the Cubs from 1909 until 1917. He was born in Dublin, Ireland, but raised in Montreal and Toronto. Archer had the best throwing arm of any catcher of the era, and he came about his renowned arm strength in an unusual manner. His right arm was severely burned in a factory accident when he fell into a vat of boiling sap at age 19. When the burns healed, the muscles in his arm shortened but became particularly strong. This allowed Archer to fire the ball to second base without rising from his squatting position from behind home plate. After his playing career, Archer worked as a hog purchaser for the Armour Meat Packing Plant. In 1931, he received a medal from the National Safety Council in Chicago for saving the lives of two men. Archer pulled both from the cab of a truck in the Chicago stockyards when they were overcome by carbon monoxide gas. He revived both with first aid.

On this date in 1918 . . .

The Cubs defeated the Phillies 2-1 in a 21-inning marathon game in Chicago. Lefty Tyler pitched a complete game for the Cubs, as did Milt Watson for the Phillies. The 21 innings by Tyler is the longest pitching performance in Cub history. The Cubs scored in the first inning, and the Phillies tied it 1-1 in the fourth. For 16 consecutive innings, from the fifth through the 20th, neither Tyler nor Watson allowed a run. In the 21st, Turner Barber pinch-hit for Rollie Zeider and singled. Watson hit Bill Killefer with a pitch, and Bill McCabe, batting for Tyler, beat out a bunt to load the bases. Max Flack then singled, his fifth hit of the afternoon, to end the contest. It is the second-longest game in Cubs history. The longest took place on May 17, 1927, when the Cubs defeated the Braves 4-3 in 22 innings in Boston. There was no scoring from the seventh inning through the 21st. In the 22nd, Hack Wilson walked, went to second on a fly ball by Riggs Stephenson and scored on Charlie Grimm's single. Bobby Smith pitched all 22 innings for the Braves. For the Cubs, starter Sheriff Blake pitched 7⅓ innings, Jim Brillheart went two-thirds of an inning and Bob Osborn pitched the final 14 innings. Osborn did not allow a run.

On this date in 1910 . . .

Franklin P. Adams' poem, "Baseball's Sad Lexicon," which made "Tinker-to-Evers-to-Chance" a national catchphrase, appeared in print for the first time in the *New York Evening Mail,* a struggling newspaper. According to baseball legend, Adams' immortalization of Tinker, Evers and Chance catapulted three mediocre infielders into the Hall of Fame. None of this is true. Adams did not make the trio famous, he wrote about them because they were already famous in 1910. Tinker, Evers and Chance were not mediocre players in their day. They were stars and played together in four World Series. If the All-Star Game had existed during their careers, it is likely that Chance would have played in five or six of them and Evers and Tinker between six and eight. Furthermore, the poem did not become well known until the 1940s when the players' Hall of Fame credentials were already firmly established in the minds of voters. The poem became famous because Adams was a well-known radio personality on the program *Information Please.* As time filler at the end of shows, Adams would often read one of his poems. It's probable that "Baseball's Sad Lexicon" was one of those read on the air and struck a chord with baseball fans.

On this date in 1912 . . .

Phillies manager Red Dooin was ejected from a game won 4-0 by Philadelphia in Chicago, for putting liniment on a baseball. The Cubs pitcher was Jimmy Lavender, whose main pitch was a spitball at a time when it was legal for pitchers to use saliva on the ball. The Phillies tried to foil Lavender by putting liniment on the ball to make it painful for Lavender to utilize the spitball. Lavender's technique was to hide the ball in his glove and lick it. The Cubs pitcher took a whiff of the ball, detected the scent of liniment and showed it to umpire Cy Rigler. The umpire tossed the ball out of play and tossed Dooin from the premises. Dooin and Lavender became involved in another dispute over a baseball on September 23, 1914, during a 9-4 loss to the Phillies in Philadelphia. Lavender attached a piece of emery board to his uniform pants and rubbed the ball against it. There was nothing in the rules in 1914 to prevent Lavender from doing so, but in the third inning, Dooin objected. Rigler strolled toward the mound, and Lavender walked into right field, refusing to be searched. The game was delayed until Lavender agreed to have the board cut off his pants.

On this date in 1978 . . .

The Cubs-Giants game at Wrigley Field was suspended because of darkness in the top of the eighth inning with San Francisco leading 9-8. The game had been interrupted three times by rain. The Giants dugout was flooded, and the team had to make their way to the playing field via the stands. The problem was solved when groundskeeper Cotton Bogren dipped his hand down and extracted a paper cup from the drain, and the water swirled out in an instant. The game was completed in San Francisco on July 28 before the regularly scheduled contest. There was no more scoring, and the Giants won 9-8.

21
July

On this date in 1951 . . .

he Cubs fired Frankie Frisch as manager and replaced him with Phil Cavarretta. Frisch had a dismal record of 141-196 with the club after being hired in June 1949. A future Hall of Famer, Frisch starred as a second baseman with the Giants and Cardinals from 1919 through 1938, and he played in eight World Series, the most of any National Leaguer in history. He was also the manager of the Cardinals from 1933 through 1938, winning a world championship in 1934. In addition, Frisch managed the Pirates from 1940 until 1946. After leaving the Pirates, Frisch vowed he was "through with managing" and went into broadcasting. He took the job with the moribund Cubs against the advice of his wife and close friends. The club was 64-90 in 1948 and 19-31 in 1949 at the time Frisch took the helm from Charlie Grimm. The Cubs lost their first six games under Frisch and showed no noticeable improvement before he was fired. He often berated his players in public with caustic remarks and was clearly unsuited to guide the youth movement the Cubs were undertaking. Frisch's players were close to open revolt over his Captain Bligh methods.

22
July

On this date in 1986 . . .

The Cubs fired ball girl Marla Collins for posing nude in *Playboy*. The 28-year-old Collins began working as a ball girl at Cubs games in 1982. Attired in shorts and a Cubs shirt, she occupied a seat near the visitors' dugout and was a familiar sight shagging fouls and keeping the umpire supplied with baseballs. Marla gained a national following among the many viewers of Cubs broadcasts on cable television and even secured her own athletic shoe endorsement, which was canceled after her appearance in *Playboy*. The eight-page spread was entitled "The Belle of the Ball Club."

On this date in 1979 . . .

The Cubs won two games against the Reds in unusual fashion. The day began with the completion of a suspended game from May 10, which was stopped at the end of the ninth inning to allow the Cubs to catch a plane. The two clubs resumed the contest in the top of the 10th on July 23, and it went nine more innings. At the conclusion, the Cubs had a 9-8 win in 18 innings. Both teams scored in the 11th. In the 18th, Ken Henderson singled, went to second on a sacrifice and scored on a single by Steve Ontiveros. In the regularly scheduled game, the Cubs won 2-1 when Dave Kingman hit a two-run, walk-off homer in the ninth.

On this date in 1972 . . .

Leo Durocher stepped down as manager, and Whitey Lockman replaced him. The Cubs had a record of 46-44 but had lost 22 of their previous 34 games and were 10 games behind the first place Pirates. Durocher and his players had been openly feuding for years as frustration grew following the team's loss to the Mets in the 1969 pennant race and the failure to win the division title in 1970 and 1971. He closed his stay in Chicago with a 535-526 record as manager, but he posted five consecutive winning seasons in six full years and another winning mark in a partial seventh season. No Cub manager prior to Durocher had back-to-back winning seasons since Charlie Grimm in 1945 and 1946. The next after Durocher to accomplish the feat was Dusty Baker in 2003 and 2004. Durocher also presided over the period in which attendance at Wrigley Field boomed, increasing by more than a million between 1966 and 1969. The five-paragraph press release issued by P. K. Wrigley announcing Durocher's departure left open the question as to whether Durocher resigned or was fired, although Wrigley acknowledged "friction between Leo and his players."

25 July

On this date in 1988 . . .

Cubs players and fans were given the opportunity to preview the new lighting system at Wrigley Field in anticipation of the first night game, scheduled for August 8. They turned the occasion into a festive affair. It began with an autograph session on the field starting at 7 p.m. and was followed by a home run hitting contest, which included retired stars Ernie Banks and Billy Williams. Then, they had batting practice. Approximately 3,000 fans paid $100 each to attend, with the gate proceeds going to charity. Shortly before sunset, the field was cleared of spectators, and at 8:45 p.m., the lights were turned on. ABC-TV, which was airing two games nationally, cut away from the telecasts to show portions of the event at Wrigley Field. Players complained that they had trouble seeing the balls in the corners of the outfield and that there was a glare at second base. With this trial run, they were able to correct the problems before the first game was played.

26 July

On this day in 1969 . . .

Leo Durocher left the club without permission during a 3-2 win over the Dodgers at Wrigley Field. It was the day before his 64th birthday, and Durocher said he was going home because of an upset stomach. A few hours later, Leo appeared in apparent good health at a parents' weekend reception at Camp Ojibwa in Eagle River, Wisconsin, some 400 miles north of Chicago. Durocher went straight from the ballpark and boarded a chartered plane at Meigs Field accompanied by his bride of five weeks. Durocher married Lynne Walker Goldblatt on June 19 in ceremonies at the Ambassador West Hotel in Chicago. Lynne was a Chicago television personality and the ex-wife of a Midwest department store executive. It was Leo's fourth marriage and Lynne's second. Her 12-year-old son was enrolled at the camp. P. K. Wrigley nearly fired Durocher over the incident. On August 13, the Cubs took an 8½-game lead over the Mets in the NL East pennant race but wound up finishing in second place, an astonishing eight games back.

On this date in 1876 . . .

Ross Barnes of the Cubs picked up six hits, including a double and a triple, in six at-bats during a 17-3 win over the Reds in Chicago. Barnes led the National League in batting that season with an average of .429. Barnes also led the league in runs (126 in only 66 games), hits (138), total bases (190) and triples (14). Barnes accumulated his high average in part because of a rule that stipulated that any ball that landed in fair territory was in play. Barnes mastered a technique in which he could maneuver a ball to land fair and immediately slice foul. After the season, a change in the rules stated that for a batted ball to be called in play by the umpires it must stay within foul lines until it crossed a base or was fielded. Barnes's batting average fell to .277 in 1877 because of the new rule and a long illness that sapped his strength. The Cubs deducted $1,000 of his $2,500 salary because of the illness, a common practice at the time. Barnes took the club to court to regain the lost income but lost the case. He also holds the distinction of hitting the first home run in National League history. It happened on May 2, 1876, during a 15-9 win over the Reds in Cincinnati.

On this date in 1977 . . .

At Wrigley Field, the Cubs and Reds combined for 11 homers to tie a National League record. Five of the home runs came in the first inning, tying another record. The Cubs won 16-15 in 13 innings. For Chicago, Bill Buckner and George Mitterwald each hit two homers, with Bobby Murcer and Jerry Morales adding one each. Pete Rose, Johnny Bench, Mike Lum, Ken Griffey, Sr. and Cesar Geronimo went deep for the Reds. Cincinnati took a 6-0 lead in the first inning, sending three deep off Ray Burris, but the Cubs went ahead 7-6 in the second. The score was 10-10 at the end of four innings. After the Reds took a 14-10 advantage, the Cubs scored three times in the eighth inning on blasts by Buckner and Morales and one in the ninth to knot the skirmish at 14-14. Steve Ontiveros tied the score with an RBI-single with two out. The Reds took a 15-14 lead in the 12th, but Mitterwald tied it 15-15 with another long ball. The Cubs won in the 13th on singles by Rick Reuschel, Ontiveros and Dave Rosello. Appearing in relief two days after a complete game shutout, Reuschel was the winning pitcher, running his record on the season to 15-3. Reuschel had a 19-5 record on August 30 and then lost five of his last six decisions to finish at 20-10 with a 2.79 ERA.

On this date in 1970 . . .

The Cubs purchased first baseman and outfielder Joe Pepitone from the Astros. One of baseball's one-of-a-kind characters during a stormy career marked by fines, suspensions, mood swings and defiance of authority figures, Pepitone became an immediate hit with young Cubs fans. His flamboyant lifestyle, long hair and "mod" outfits kept his admirers entertained. He was the first player to bring a hair dryer into the clubhouse at a time when a man using a hair dryer was considered an embarrassment. He had previously played on three World Series teams with the Yankees but had never quite reached his potential. In 1970 and 1971, Pepitone had 640 at-bats as a Cub and contributed with a .294 batting average, 28 homers and 105 RBIs. But those who buck tradition are tolerated only when they play well, and things began to go south in 1972 when Pepitone lost playing time, had a running battle with manager Leo Durocher and sat out two months on the voluntarily retired list. The Cubs traded Pepitone to the Braves in May 1973.

On this date in 1962 . . .

The American League won the All-Star Game 9-4 before a crowd of 38,359 at Wrigley Field. It was the second of two All-Star Games played in 1962 (there were two All-Star Games each season from 1959 through 1962). Rocky Colavito of the Tigers, Pete Runnels of the Red Sox, Leon Wagner of the Angels and Johnny Roseboro of the Dodgers each hit home runs. P. K. Wrigley was not at the game, however, and instead watched the game on television from his retreat in Lake Geneva, Wisconsin. Wrigley claimed his presence at Wrigley Field "wasn't necessary." There have been two other All-Star Games at the Cubs' ballpark. The American League won 2-1 on July 8, 1947, before 41,123 spectators. Johnny Mize of the Giants put the NL on top 1-0 in the fourth inning, but the AL came back with a run in the sixth inning and another in the seventh. Stan Spence of the Senators drove in the winning run with a single. The AL was also victorious at Wrigley by a 2-0 score on July 10, 1990, before 39,071. The NL was held to only two hits. Both runs scored in the seventh inning on a double by Julio Franco of the Rangers.

31
July

The question of the day.

Who was Billy Jurges?

A fiery shortstop, Jurges played for the Cubs from 1931 through 1938 and again in 1946 and 1947. The most bizarre incident involving Jurges happened on July 6, 1932, when a 21-year-old dancer named Violet Popovich Valli shot Jurges with a .25-caliber pistol in Chicago's Carlos Hotel. Valli was a former girlfriend of Jurges who was angry because he broke off the relationship. She appeared in his room with a gun, and Jurges was wounded trying to wrestle the weapon away from her. In the struggle, one bullet caromed off Jurges's ribs and exited near his right shoulder. Another slug grazed the little finger of his left hand. The wounds were superficial, and Jurges was back in the lineup in 17 days. He refused to press charges, though, because he was convinced that Valli had not intended to shoot him. Valli used her notoriety as part of her act, signing a 22-week contract to sing in local nightclubs and theaters. She was billed as Violet "What I Did For Love" Valli, the "Most Talked About Girl in Chicago."

Wrigley Hits 100

August

01 August

The question of the day.

How many Cubs players have collected six hits in a game?

Cal McVey (July 22, 1976, and July 25, 1876)
Ross Barnes (July 25, 1876)
George Gore (May 7, 1880)
Barry McCormick (June 29, 1897)
Frank Demaree (July 5, 1937)
Don Kessinger (June 17, 1971)
Bill Madlock (July 26, 1975)
Jose Cardenal (May 2, 1976)
Sammy Sosa (July 2, 1993)

All have collected six hits in a game for the Cubs. McVey is the only player in major league history with back-to-back six-hit games. The only other players with two games of six hits or more in a career are Jimmie Foxx in 1930 and 1932 and Kirby Puckett in 1987 and 1991. Barnes' six-hit performance was the third consecutive game that a Cubs batter collected six hits.

02 August

On this date in 1894 . . .

A replacement ball led to a protest in a game between the Cubs and the Louisville Colonels in Louisville. In the fifth inning, Walt Wilmot of the Cubs knocked a foul ball over the fence. Louisville wanted the ball retrieved and put back into play--in the 19th century, one ball was often used the entire game. However, a new ball was tossed to the Louisville pitcher. New balls introduced in the middle of a game always caused controversy because it was thought they traveled farther when hit and gave the team at bat the advantage. When the Cubs scored four runs in the fifth, three of them with the new ball, and won 4-3, Louisville manager Billy Barnie filed a protest. The league later denied his claim, but the following day, the conflict over baseballs continued. Cap Anson refused to play with the balls Louisville furnished, claiming they were an inferior lot left over from the previous year. Anson walked to the plate and handed a box of balls to umpire Tom Lynch with a message from NL President Nick Young stating they should be used in the game. Barnie refused to play with the balls, citing a league rule that stipulated the home team had the right to provide the balls. Lynch agreed and forfeited the game to the Colonels.

On this date in 1923 . . .

Shortstop Charlie Hollocher left the Cubs and did not return until spring training in 1924. He left a note in the clubhouse addressed to manager Bill Killefer. Hollocher wrote: "Feeling pretty rotten so made up my mind to go home and take a rest and forget baseball the rest of the year." Hollocher had one of the strangest careers in baseball history. His career was beset by a series of mishaps. In 1919, Hollocher missed three weeks with an injured thumb, then was hit in the head by a line drive during batting practice and knocked unconscious. Two weeks later, he was running between second and third base when a batted ball struck him in the neck. In 1921, a bad hop off of a ground ball broke his nose. In 1923, he missed the first four weeks of the season with the flu and was in and out of the lineup with a mysterious stomach ailment before leaving the club. Hollocher continued to battle stomach problems, but physicians could find nothing wrong with him. He retired after the 1924 season, convinced that baseball was ruining his health. It is open conjecture whether Hollocher was suffering from hypochondria, mental illness or an undiagnosed ailment. He died in 1940 from a self-inflicted gunshot wound to the neck.

On this date in 1960 . . .

Reds second baseman Billy Martin punched Cubs pitcher Jim Brewer in the face during a brawl at Wrigley Field. Playing in only his fifth big-league game, Brewer suffered a fracture of the orbit bone around the right eye. Brewer touched off the incident in the second inning with a high, inside pitch that caused Martin to hit the dirt. Martin swung at the next pitch, but the bat slipped out of his hands and sailed toward the mound, landing about 15 feet from Brewer. Martin walked out to retrieve the bat, and after an exchange of words, the two began swinging at each other. On August 5, Martin was fined $500 and suspended for five days by NL President Warren Giles. Two weeks later, Brewer and the Cubs hit Martin with a $1,040,000 damage suit, prompting Martin's classic response, "How do they want it? Cash or check?" The claim was settled out of court six years later, with Martin paying an amount reported to be between $10,000 and $25,000.

On this date in 1894 . . .

A fire broke out in the grandstand at West Side Grounds with the Cubs leading the Reds 8-1 in the sixth inning. Fans occupied every available seat in the grandstand and bleachers of the wooden ballpark, with a crowd of about 10,000. Suddenly a cry of "Fire!" was heard from the bleachers, and a thin veil of smoke crept through the seats from below. Panicked fans jammed the four exits, with hundreds injured as the stampeding fans tore down four rows of barbed wire that had been put up in front of the stands to prevent fans from mobbing the umpire. Many became entangled in the wire as they tried to crawl through and were caught as the fire edged closer. When the fire department arrived, the stands on the first base side were a mass of flames, and the firemen were unable to contain the blaze. The wooden sidewalks on Lincoln Street (now Wolcott Street) along the first base side of the stands also caught fire. Fortunately, two hospitals were nearby to treat the wounded. The cause was variously reported as a cigar stub put into a garbage can or as being from a plumber's stove. Much of the third base side of the ballpark was saved, and they played a game there the following day.

On this date in 1929 . . .

The Cubs lost 5-4 to the Dodgers at Wrigley Field in near-riot conditions. At the time, the ballpark admitted women for free on designated days, and nearly 29,000 ladies showed that day. Combined with at least that number of men, the ticket takers and turnstile keepers were overpowered before the gates were locked, leaving at least 10,000 fans outside. The crowd overran the playing field, stood in the aisles and sat atop the outfield fences. Some newspapers estimated that there was 65,000 people inside Wrigley Field.

On this date in 1906 . . .

The Cubs won by forfeit when the Giants refused to admit umpire John Johnstone into the Polo Grounds in New York. When he showed up for the game, the gatekeeper barred Johnstone from entering and told him that police inspector James Sweeney could not ensure his safety. New York manager John McGraw had orchestrated the incident. Neither Sweeney nor the city police had any knowledge of it. Inside the ballpark, the second umpire Bob Emslie refused to work without Johnstone. According to National League rules of the day, if no umpires were available, each club appointed a player to serve as umpire. McGraw designated Giants player Sammy Strang, but Cubs manager Frank Chance refused to play the game without Johnstone or Emslie. Strang then awarded his team a victory by forfeit. Meanwhile, on the outside, Johnstone awarded the Cubs the victory by forfeit. The crowd of 11,000 chanting "Play Ball! Play Ball!" was sent home. The next day, NL President Harry Pulliam awarded the game to the Cubs by forfeit. He also backed Johnstone and assigned him to the August 7 game between the Giants and Cubs. The fans applauded the umpires, and this time the teams settled the game on the field, with the Cubs winning 3-2.

On this date in 1988 . . .

The Cubs, formed three years before Thomas Edison's invention of the light bulb, introduced night baseball at Wrigley field, ushering in a new era and ending decades of tradition. The atmosphere was akin to the World Series, Mardi Gras and New Year's Eve rolled into one. There were 1.8 million phone calls made to the Cubs' ticket office on the day the 8,000 remaining tickets went on sale. A total of 558 media credentials were issued, by far the most ever for a regular-season game. The previous record was 275 issued by the Reds in 1985 when Pete Rose broke Ty Cobb's career hit record. The crowd of 39,008 included many celebrities and politicians. WGN-TV drew a huge nationwide audience. At 6:09 p.m., 91-year-old Harry Grossman, a retired tire dealer who attended his first Cubs game in 1906, threw the switch that turned on the lights. The game began at 7:01 p.m., and the Cubs led 3-1 in the fourth when rain stopped play at 10:25 p.m. The first official night game at Wrigley Field was played the following evening with the Cubs defeating the Mets 6-4. Although NBC-TV carried the game nationally, the fanfare of the previous night was absent, along with many of the politicians and celebrities.

09 August

On this date in 1942 . . .

The Cubs won a wild, 18-inning game against Cincinnati, ultimately beating the Reds 10-8. The Cubs led 4-0 with a Reds runner on third base and two out in the ninth when shortstop Bobby Sturgeon dropped what should have been a game-ending pop-up. Before the inning was over, the Reds tied the score 4-4. The Cubs scored two in the tenth, but the Reds matched it in their half of the inning. Chicago surged ahead once more with two runs in the 12th for an 8-6 lead, and again, the Reds tied the score. After a one hour rain delay, the two clubs battled until the 18th, when the Cubs scored two runs that the Reds were unable to counter.

10 August

On this date in 1883 . . .

Cubs manager Cap Anson refused to play an exhibition contest against Toledo, of the Northwestern League, if Toledo's African American player Moses Walker appeared in the game. Toledo management noted that the team had played many major league clubs without incident and declared it would play Walker regardless of Anson's objections. Anson backed down, Walker played right field and the Cubs won 7-6 in 10 innings. A year later, Toledo joined the American Association, and Walker and his brother Welday became the first African Americans in the majors. The Cubs played another exhibition game in Toledo in 1884, and Anson gained a written guarantee before signing the contract that the Walker brothers would not play. This time, Toledo agreed, and the Walkers sat out that contest and all future Cubs' appearances in the northern Ohio city. Toledo dropped out of the American Association after the 1884 campaign, and Moses and Welday Walker were the last African Americans in the majors until the arrival of Jackie Robinson in 1947.

On this date in 1884 . . .

A crowd of 2,000 in Chicago watched the Cubs lose by forfeit in the first game and play to a tie in the second game of a double-header against Buffalo. In the first inning of the first game, Cubs outfielder George Gore was on first base when King Kelly hit a grounder to second baseman Hardy Richardson. After Gore was forced out at second, he threw his arms around Richardson to prevent him from completing the double play. Umpire Stewart Decker declared both Gore and Kelly out. Manager Cap Anson objected, claiming Kelly could not be called out for Gore's indiscretion. After a long argument, Anson pulled his team off the field, and Decker forfeited the game to Buffalo. After a half-hour wait, Anson decided to play the second game, a make-up of a postponed contest from earlier in the season. After nine innings, the game was called on account of darkness with the score 6-6.

On this date in 1912 . . .

NL President Thomas Lynch suspended Johnny Evers for five games. The previous day, during an 11-10 win over the Braves in Boston, Evers and umpire William Finneran exchanged blows following an argument over one of Finneran's calls. The suspension meant that Evers had to miss the first two games of a crucial three-game series against the Giants that began on August 15. At the time, the Cubs were 6½ games behind the Giants and gaining ground. Cubs President Charles Murphy blasted Lynch for the suspension, claiming that Lynch was a mere puppet of Giants owner John Brush. Murphy also accused the Cardinals, managed by former Giant Roger Bresnahan, of underachieving against the Giants. Later, Phillies owner Horace Fogel, who was seen as a front for Murphy, echoed the accusation against Bresnahan and accused NL umpires of fixing the pennant race for the Giants in a letter sent to Murphy. Murphy then turned the letter over to the *Chicago Post* for publication. At a league meeting on November 27, the other owners drummed Fogel out of baseball. No charges were made against Murphy, but NL owners, tired of his antics, forced him to sell his stock in the Cubs in February 1914.

13 August

On this date in 1879 . . .

The Cubs won a forfeit against the Reds in Cincinnati. At the start of the 3 p.m. game, it was raining steadily, and the field was muddy. Reds manager Cal McVey declared the field unplayable, but Chicago skipper Cap Anson insisted the two teams play to avoid issuing refunds, even though only 165 spectators had paid admission. At the time, umpires did not travel from city to city. The umpires assigned to games lived in the city where the contest was played. According to the NL rules of 1879, the visiting team submitted a list of five umpires, the home team narrowed the list to two and the visiting team chose between the remaining two. Anson refused to accept any of the men nominated by the Reds and appointed Cubs employee John A. Brown as umpire of the game. Brown then declared the game a forfeit because the Reds refused to play. At a league meeting the following December, it was declared a legal Chicago victory.

14 August

The question of the day.

Who was Pat Malone?

As a 25-year-old rookie with the Cubs in 1928, Pat Malone lost his first seven decisions but finished at 18-13. He won 22 games in 1929 and 20 more in 1930. Malone was unable to continue his success, however, because he loved the nightlife and was a frequent drinking partner of Hack Wilson in many of Chicago's illegal drinking establishments during Prohibition. Malone's given name was Perce Lee Malone, and during the 1928 season, his roommate on the road was Percy Lee Jones. Despite the similarities in names, Perce Lee and Percy Lee were not a match made in heaven. The arrangement ended when Malone trapped some pigeons off the ledge of their hotel room and placed them in the bed of the sleeping Jones. On September 6, 1931, Malone cornered writers Harold Johnson of the *Chicago Evening American* and Wayne Otto of the *Chicago Herald and Examiner* in the vestibule between two train cars and slugged both in the face. Neither writer had a chance to defend himself. Wilson stood by and encouraged Malone to beat up the scribes. The club fined Malone $500 because of the fight. For this and other incidents, the Cubs suspended Wilson without pay for the rest of the season.

The question of day.

Who did Hack Wilson fight in a train station in 1929?

Two years earlier, Wilson also had trouble in the vicinity of trains, battling two players from the Reds in separate incidents in a single day. During a double-header against the Reds at Wrigley Field on July 4, Wilson fought Reds pitcher Ray Kolp. Kolp, whose nickname was Jockey for his ability to insult opponents, had been heckling Wilson mercilessly, and in the sixth inning of the second game, the Cubs slugger could take no more. After hitting a single, Wilson turned and headed toward the Reds dugout, planting a right hook to Kolp's jaw. Wilson neglected to call time out and was tagged out by Cincinnati third baseman Charlie Dressen. Later that evening at Union Station, where both teams were boarding a train, Wilson sought out Kolp to either apologize or fight. Pete Donahue, another Cincinnati pitcher, made some unkind remarks about Wilson's behavior at the ballpark, and Hack punched him twice in the face, sparking a brawl between the two. Wilson had to have two stitches to his lip and was suspended for three days by National League President John Heydler.

On this date in 1890 . . .

The Cubs scored 13 times in the fifth inning and defeated the Pirates 18-5 in Chicago. The Cubs set a major league record, since tied, by hitting two grand slams in the inning. Malachi Kittridge and Tom Burns each hit one off of Pittsburgh hurler Bill Phillips. This is the only time in Cubs history that two players have hit grand slams in a single inning. The only other time that two Cubs batters hit grand slams in the same game was during a 22-7 win over the Astros on June 3, 1987, at Wrigley Field. Those were hit by Brian Dayett in the first inning and Keith Moreland in the sixth. The two clubs combined to tie a big-league mark with three grand slams that afternoon. Houston's Billy Hatcher sent a Rick Sutcliffe pitch deep in the fourth with the bases loaded. The Cubs scored nine runs in the first inning during the rout. Moreland hit a second homer and drove in seven runs. Jim Sundberg, Ryne Sandberg and Andre Dawson also homered. Jody Davis scored five of the 22 Chicago runs.

17
August

On this date in 1982 . . .

Officials suspended the Cubs-Dodgers game at Wrigley Field because of darkness at the end of the 17th inning with the score 1-1. The Cubs scored in the first inning and the Dodgers in the second. They completed it the next day and went 21 innings before the Dodgers won 2-1. Dusty Baker drove in the winning run with a sacrifice fly off Allen Ripley, scoring Steve Sax on a close play at the plate. Eight Los Angeles pitchers and six Cubs hurlers combined for 18 consecutive scoreless innings between the third and the 20th. Both managers were ejected, as well as Cubs coach John Vukovich, who was serving as the acting manager. The Dodgers used all 25 players, and pitchers Fernando Valenzuela and Bob Welch played in the outfield. The Dodgers also won the regularly scheduled game 7-4.

18
August

On this date in 1907 . . .

The grandstand caught fire prior to a Cubs exhibition game in Bridgeport, Connecticut. The fire broke out while the Cubs were warming up. A cigarette dropped into a pile of garbage under the bleachers started the blaze. By the time the fire was extinguished 40 minutes later, the grandstand was almost a total loss. Fortunately, the 5,000 in attendance escaped unharmed. To avoid disappointing the fans, the Cubs played a five-inning game and won 3-1. A total of 10,000 watched the contest as another 5,000 curious onlookers had joined to the original attendees. Several foul balls landed in the still-smoldering ruins.

On this date in 1969 . . .

Ken Holtzman pitched a no-hitter to defeat the Braves at Wrigley Field. He threw 112 pitches, walking three batters and surprisingly striking out no one. The 16 mile an hour wind blowing toward home plate that day helped Holtzman's effort, keeping a seventh-inning drive by Hank Aaron in the ballpark. Billy Williams caught it against the vines in left field. In the ninth, Holtzman retired Felipe Alou on a fly ball to short-center field caught by shortstop Don Kessinger, Felix Millan on a grounder to Ron Santo at first base and Aaron on a ground ball to second baseman Glenn Beckert. Randy Hundley had missed the start that day because of an injured thumb. The starting catcher for Holtzman's no-hitter was Bill Heath, who caught only nine games as a Cub. Heath had to leave the game, however, when he broke his hand on a foul tip. Gene Oliver replaced him. Heath never caught another game in the big leagues.

On this date in 1974 . . .

Carmen Fanzone hit a grand slam in the eighth inning off of Charlie Hough, but the Cubs lost 18-8 to the Dodgers at Wrigley Field. Fanzone entered the game in the sixth as a defensive replacement at third base for Bill Madlock after the Dodgers built an 18-2 lead. Fanzone played for the Cubs from 1971 through 1974. He was also a professional trumpet player. In fact, Fanzone's first appearance on the playing field at Wrigley Field was with Central Michigan University's marching band as part of the halftime show at Bears games in both 1963 and 1964. Before one Cubs game, he played the National Anthem on the trumpet. Later, Fanzone played trumpet in Johnny Carson's *Tonight Show band*.

21 August

On this date in 1975 . . .

Rick and Paul Reuschel became the first pair of brothers in major league history to combine on a shutout. Rick pitched the first 6⅓ innings but had to leave the game because of a blister on his finger. Paul went the final 2⅔ innings to give the Cubs a 7-0 win over the Dodgers at Wrigley Field. At six feet three inches tall and a hefty 235 pounds, Rick Reuschel bore little resemblance to a professional athlete but posted a 135-127 record for the Cubs, mostly on subpar teams. He lasted 20 years in the majors. On the Cubs all-time lists of pitching leaders, Rick ranks 12th in victories, eighth in games pitched (358), second in games started (343), sixth in innings pitched (2,290) and third in strikeouts (1,367). The Cubs traded Reuschel to the Yankees on June 12, 1981, in a deal that worked out to the Cubs' disadvantage. He won 79 more games after he left Chicago for a total of 214 for his career before calling it quits in 1991 at age 42. Reuschel pitched in the World Series for the Yankees in 1981 and the Giants in 1989. Rick and Paul were teammates with the Cubs from 1975 through 1978. Paul was a relief pitcher and posted a 12-11 record with 12 saves while with the Cubs.

22 August

On this date in 2003 . . .

Carlos Zambrano carried a no-hitter into the eighth inning, and Sammy Sosa hit his 499th and 500th homers as a Cub. The Cubs won 4-1 over the Diamondbacks in Phoenix. With two out in the eighth, Shea Hillenbrand dropped a ball down the third base line. Aramis Ramirez charged it and made a throw to first, but umpire Kevin Kelley called Hillenbrand safe to end Zambrano's no-hit bid. TV replays showed that Hillenbrand was out. In the ninth, however, Zambrano gave up two more hits and a run. Both of Sosa's homers were hit off of Curt Schilling.

On this date in 1971 . . .

Prior to a 6-3 win over the Reds at Wrigley Field, Cubs manager Leo Durocher and his players squared off in an acrimonious clubhouse meeting. Durocher ripped into Milt Pappas for letting Doug Rader of the Astros hit an 0-2 pitch for a double to drive in the winning run in a 4-3 loss the previous day. After Durocher spoke, he told the players they were free to air their grievances. Joe Pepitone came to Pappas's defense. "He didn't want to do it," Pepitone said. "Why are you always blaming people?" Anger and tension, which had been building for years over Durocher's handling of the team, bubbled to the surface. Other players also spoke up, defiantly blasting the Cubs manager. Durocher responded by ripping into the players one by one in a profanity-laden harangue on what he believed were their deficiencies. Durocher's relationship with his players was irretrievably damaged. P. K. Wrigley brought Durocher back in 1972, but he was dismissed on July 24 of that season.

On this date in 1905 . . .

Cubs pitcher Ed Reulbach pitched 20 innings to defeat the Phillies 2-1 in Philadelphia. Tully Sparks also pitched 20 innings in a losing effort. Both teams scored their first run in the 13th inning. In the winning 20th inning, Jack McCarthy singled, took second on Doc Casey's sacrifice and scored on Frank Chance's single. It was the second time in 1905 that Reulbach pitched a marathon game. He hurled 18 innings to beat the Cardinals 2-1 in St. Louis on June 24. Reulbach's most impressive performance came on September 26, 1908. In the thick of a nail-biting pennant race with the Giants and Pirates, he pitched two complete-game, nine-inning shutouts in the same day, defeating the Dodgers 5-0 and 3-0 in Brooklyn.

Reulbach allowed only five hits in the first game, three in the second and issued just one walk in the 18 innings. The two games lasted two hours and 52 minutes. Reulbach is the only pitcher in major league history to pitch two shutouts in one day, a distinction that will likely last forever.

On this date in 1922 . . .

The highest-scoring game in major league history was played when the Cubs beat the Phillies 26-23 in Chicago. There were 51 hits, another record by two teams in a nine-inning game, 26 of them by the Phillies. The hits included 34 singles, 12 doubles, two triples and three home runs. In addition, there were 10 errors by 10 different players and 21 walks. The Phillies left 16 men on base, and the Cubs stranded nine. Chicago scored 10 runs in the second inning to take an 11-3 lead and 14 in the fourth to pull ahead 25-6. The Cubs had a 26-9 advantage after seven innings before the Phillies plated eight runs in the eighth inning and six in the ninth. Philadelphia had the bases loaded when the game ended on a Tiny Osborne strikeout of Bevo LeBourveau. Pitchers Jimmy Ring and Lefty Weinert of the Phillies and Tony Kaufman (the winning pitcher), George Stueland, Ed Morris, Uel Eubanks and Osborne for the Cubs absorbed the beating. It was Eubanks's second big-league game. He never pitched in the majors again.

On this date in 1929 . . .

The Cubs defeated the Reds 9-5 at Wrigley Field on a freak grand slam home run by Norm McMillan. In the eighth inning with the score 5-5 and the bases loaded with Cubs, McMillan hit a Rube Ehrhardt pitch down the left-field line. Reds left fielder Evar Swanson saw the ball hit an open gutter running along the base of the stands, then lost sight of the ball. He looked in and around the gutter and began to wonder if the horsehide had disappeared into thin air. The frantic Swanson spotted the jacket of Cubs pitcher Ken Penner, who was warming up in the bullpen. The Cincinnati outfielder shook the jacket, but still failed to locate the ball. By this time, all of the runners had crossed the plate, and the search ended. At the start of the ninth inning, Penner entered the game and put on the jacket for the trip from the bullpen to the mound. As he placed his right hand into the sleeve, he found the baseball that Swanson had been looking for in vain. Home runs such as this were no longer possible after the end of the 1930 season due to a rules change. After 1930, balls that bounced into the stands or into an obstruction, such as Penner's jacket, were ground rule doubles.

On this date in 1956 . . .

Ernie Banks returned to the lineup after missing 18 games with an infected hand. The hand ailment caused him to miss his first game since his major league debut in 1953. Banks set a still-standing MLB record for most consecutive games played at the start of a career with 424. The August 27, 1956, contest started another consecutive games streak that reached 717 games before it was snapped in 1961.

The question of the day.

How did the 1968 Democratic Convention in Chicago affect the Cubs?

Clashes between demonstrators protesting the Vietnam War and Chicago police marked the convention to nominate Hubert Humphrey as the Democratic presidential candidate. It resulted in hundreds of arrests and injuries over a period of four days. Cubs pitcher Ken Holtzman was among the Illinois National Guard troops called to active duty in an attempt to quell the violence. The Cubs were playing in Los Angeles during the early part of the convention but returned on Thursday, August 29 for a series against the Astros at Wrigley Field as demonstrators and police were still battling on the streets. On August 30, Houston players spent a few nervous moments passing through the barricades set up by protesters. Arriving at the Conrad Hilton Hotel, the Astros found themselves in the middle of chemical warfare between demonstrators using stink bombs and police using tear gas.

29 August

On this date in 1989 . . .

Down 9-0 to the Astros, the Cubs staged an incredible comeback to win 10-9 in 10 innings at Wrigley Field. The Cubs scored two in the sixth but still down seven runs, all looked lost. Manager Don Zimmer took out Andre Dawson for a rest and replaced him in right field with Dwight Smith, who would contribute greatly in eliminating the deficit with runs batted in in three consecutive plate appearances. Three scored in the seventh on a two-run single by Lloyd McClendon and an RBI-single from Smith. The Cubs tied the score with four in the eighth. Ryne Sandberg, McClendon and Mark Grace drove in runs with singles, and Smith plated the tying run with a sacrifice fly. The winning run scored in the 10th on a walk by Jerome Walton and singles by McClendon and Smith.

30 August

On this date in 1940 . . .

The Cubs purchased outfielder Lou Novikoff from the Los Angeles Angels of the Pacific Coast League for $100,000. Novikoff never lived up to his billing as a player, but he became one of the most off-beat players ever to wear a Cubs uniform. Nicknamed "The Mad Russian," Novikoff was born in Glendale, Arizona. He was one of 12 children and spoke only Russian until he was 10. Novikoff was a harmonica virtuoso, had a booming baritone voice and had been a "strongman" and a strip-tease performer before playing baseball. Novikoff could hit, but his fielding, throwing and base running were atrocious. There was no end to his excuses for his deficiencies. Novikoff complained he could not play left field at Wrigley Field because the foul lines were crooked, and he was afraid that the ivy on the outfield walls was poisonous. He also claimed he could not hit on the road because he was unable to eat a Russian dish of hamburger and cabbage called "Hoopsa" that his wife Esther made for him. Novikoff even blamed the club's light-weight uniforms for the their losing record. He played in Chicago from 1941 through 1944 and hit .282 with 15 home runs in 1,058 at-bats.

31
August

On this date in 1896...

A popular legend was born. In the bottom of the 10th inning of a scoreless game between the Cubs and Senators in Washington, Cubs outfielder Bill Lange made a diving somersault catch off the bat of Gene DeMontreville. During the same inning, Cubs first baseman George Decker broke his wrist on a throw from third baseman Barry McCormick. Because there was a hospital adjacent to the ballpark, Washington outfielder Kip Selbach used a ladder as a battering ram to knock down several boards of the outfield fence to give Decker a convenient exit. This led to the legend that Lange crashed through the fence, catching Selbach's hit. The Senators won the game 1-0 in 11 innings. Just three years later, Lange announced his retirement from baseball at age 28. At six foot one and 190 pounds, Lange was a huge man for his time, and today would be called a "five-tool" player. In seven seasons in the majors, all with the Cubs, Lange hit .330, stole 400 bases and played stellar defense in center field. He quit at the peak of his career to wed the daughter of a San Francisco real estate magnate who forbid her to marry a ballplayer. Lange refused all comeback offers once he left the game.

Wrigley Hits 100

September

01
September

The question of the day.

How long have Cubs fans been watching games from outside of the ballpark?

The tradition dates to at least 1882 when newspapers reported that approximately 1,000 people viewed the home opener on May 10 at Lakefront Park, located at Michigan and Randolph Streets, for free from a nearby viaduct that overlooked the field. Cubs officials unsuccessfully attempted to eliminate what they called an "unfair opportunity to beat the gate" by petitioning City Council to pass a law banning people from stopping on the viaduct during games, but the council rejected the petition. The Cubs responded by building a 37½-foot-high fence to block views from the viaduct. On June 24, 1884, a Chicago judge ruled the Cubs had to take down their fence at the end of the season. A suit against the club claimed the barrier illegally blocked the lake view and prevented landowners to the west from enjoying the benefits of lake breezes. At the end of the season, the Cubs closed Lakefront Park and moved to a new ballpark on the West Side.

02
September

On this date in 1878 . . .

The Cubs and the Boston Braves played an exhibition game in Chicago to benefit victims of a yellow fever epidemic that claimed the lives of approximately 20,000 people in the Mississippi River Valley. They raised a total of $682. Albert Spalding pitched for Chicago, and 43-year-old Harry Wright was on the mound for Boston. Wright was Boston's manager and was one of the founders of the 1869 Cincinnati Red Stockings, baseball's first professional team. Wright had not played regularly for eight years, but he beat Spalding and the Cubs 10-5. The Cubs won another exhibition game against Boston in Chicago on September 16 to test a new rule where players received a walk after six balls. In 1878, it took nine balls for a walk. At the conclusion of the season, the nine-ball walk remained on the books. During the 1880s, the league gradually reduced the number of balls necessary for a walk until it reached the four-ball format in 1889.

On this date in 1970 . . .

Billy Williams sat out a game for the first time since 1963, ending his streak of consecutive games played at 1,117. The Cubs beat the Phillies 7-2 at Wrigley Field. Cleo James played left field in William's place. Williams said that the streak had gone far enough and that he wanted to end the pressure and "get the monkey off my back." He returned to the lineup the next day and did not miss another game for the rest of the season. Williams remained remarkably durable. He missed just five games in 1971, six in 1972 and five in 1973. At the time, Williams had the third longest consecutive games streak in baseball history, trailing only Lou Gehrig (2,130 games) and Everett Scott (1,307). Williams has since been passed by Cal Ripken, Jr. (2,632), Steve Garvey (1,207) and Miguel Tejada (1,152). Billy played for the Cubs from 1959 through 1974. On the all-time club lists, he ranks third in games (2,213), third in at-bats (8,479), second in total bases (4,262), third in home runs (392), third in RBIs (1,353), third in hits (2,510), fourth in runs (1,306), fifth in doubles (402), fifth in walks (911), seventh in slugging percentage (.503) and eighth in triples (87).

On this date in 1891 . . .

Making light of being referred to as an "old man" repeatedly in the press, 39-year-old Cap Anson wore a shaggy, gray wig and a long, gray false beard during a 5-3 win over Boston in Chicago. Anson wore the "grandpa" costume throughout the entire contest. However, it did not help him at the plate, as Anson went hitless in four at-bats. Despite his age, Anson played in 136 of Chicago's 137 games in 1891 and hit .291 with a league-leading 120 RBIs. He went on to play six more seasons in the majors.

On this date . . .

The Red Sox defeated the Cubs 1-0 in game one of the 1918 World Series before 19,274 at Comiskey Park. Babe Ruth pitched a complete game six-hitter. The losing pitcher was Hippo Vaughn, who also yielded only six hits. The lone run of the game scored in the fourth inning on a single by Stuffy McInnis. During the game, a fight broke out when Red Sox coach Heinie Wagner, insulted by Vaughn's taunting, charged the Cubs dugout. Because of World War I, they played the Series in early September. The regular season ended on September 2 to comply with an order issued by the federal government requiring all men of draft age to either enter the military service or find a war-related job. September 5 is the earliest date a World Series game has ever been played. Comiskey Park held game one instead of the Cubs' home, Weeghman Park. That decision seems unthinkable today. The stands at Weeghman Park held only about 16,000, while Comiskey could comfortably hold twice that many. None of the games were sellouts, however, as the war mitigated interest in baseball. The game was also the scene of the first pre-game flyover by military personnel when 60 Army airplanes flew over the field in formation.

On this date in 1883 . . .

The Cubs set a major league record by scoring 18 runs in the seventh inning during a 26-6 win over Detroit in Chicago. The Cubs also established records for most hits (18) and total bases (29) in an inning. A total of 23 batters went to the plate. Tom Burns, Fred Pfeffer and Ned Williamson each had three hits and scored three runs in the inning to set two more major league marks. Burns collected two doubles and a home run, and Pfeffer and Williamson both managed two singles and a double.

07 September

On this date in 1998 . . .

During a 3-2 Cardinals win over the Cubs in St. Louis, Mark McGwire hit his 61st home run of the season to tie the all-time record for most home runs in a season set by Roger Maris in 1961. Sammy Sosa entered the game with 58 home runs. McGwire struck his record-tying blast in the first inning off Mike Morgan. McGwire hugged his 10-year-old son Matthew, who arrived 30 minutes before game time. Also in attendance were McGwire's parents. His father John was celebrating his 61st birthday on the day Mark hit his 61st homer. The six children of the late Roger Maris also were among those in the stands. After hitting the homer, McGwire saluted in their direction. The next day, McGwire passed Maris with his 62nd home run, a blast off Steve Trachsel of the Cubs during the Cardinals 6-3 win in St. Louis. After rounding the bases, McGwire shook hands with Cubs infielders and catcher Scott Servais. Once again, McGwire paused to lift his son in the air and was hugged by Sosa, his friendly rival. McGwire went to the front row of the stands to embrace the Maris family. At the end of the season, McGwire had 70 home runs, and Sosa had 66.

08 September

On this date in 1985 . . .

Pete Rose tied Ty Cobb in a game between the Reds and the Cubs at Wrigley Field. At game time, Rose had 4,189 career hits, two short of Cobb's record of 4,191. Rose was not planning to play the game because Cubs southpaw Steve Trout was the starting pitcher, and Rose had not started against Trout all season. Trout was scratched after he injured his pitching elbow falling off a bicycle the night before, however, and Rose, Cincinnati's player-manager, penciled himself into the starting lineup against the right-handed Steve Patterson. Rose collected hit number 4,190 with a single in the first inning, and tied Cobb's all-time hit record in the fifth with another single off Patterson. Pete went to the plate twice more and failed to collect a hit. The game ended in a 5-5 tie after nine innings because of darkness. Rose broke the record with a single off Eric Show of the Padres on September 11. Later, a game-by-game accounting of Cobb's career revealed he collected 4,189 hits instead of 4,191. This meant Rose actually broke the record in Chicago on September 8, 1985. Rose tied Cobb's revised figure with hit number 4,189 on a single off Patterson in the sixth inning of a 7-5 loss to the Reds at Wrigley Field on September 6.

09
September

On this date in 1931 . . .

With the country in the grip of the Great Depression, the Cubs defeated the White Sox 3-0 in a charity exhibition game before 34,865 at Comiskey Park to benefit the unemployed. The teams turned over a total of $44,489 to the Illinois State Unemployment Fund. Notorious gangster Al Capone, a White Sox fan, sat in the front row with his bodyguard. Before the first game of the City Series against the White Sox at Wrigley Field on September 30, Cubs catcher Gabby Hartnett was photographed with Capone while signing a ball for Capone's son. When Commissioner Kenesaw Landis saw the photo, he issued an edict barring players from fraternizing with fans at the ballpark. Soon, Capone would not be available for any photos at Chicago ballparks. On October 17, he was convicted of tax evasion. Capone spent the next eight years in federal prisons in Atlanta and on Alcatraz Island before dying in Miami in 1947.

10
September

On this day in 1918 . . .

The players of both the Cubs and the Boston Red Sox threatened to strike, delaying the start of game five of the World Series at Fenway Park. The players were angry because the winners' and losers' share of the gate receipts had been drastically reduced. The players' share that season was less than a third of what it had been in previous years. Attendance at the games was lower than normal because of World War I. Ticket prices were decreased, and baseball earmarked part of the gate money for wartime charities. Also the second-, third- and fourth-place clubs received part of the loot for the first time. Negotiations were held with the National Commission. The players wanted a guarantee of $2,000 to the winning team and $1,400 to the losing team, figures that were only a little more than half of what the participants in the 1917 Fall Classic received. The National Commission was unmoved. The players finally backed off their demands and the threats to strike, not wanting to appear greedy while the nation was at war. The Cubs won 3-0. The Red Sox winning share of the Series was only $671 per player while the Cubs received just $1,103. In 1919, the winning and losing shares were $5,207 and $3,254, respectively.

11
September

On this date in 1969 . . .

The Cubs endured a heartbreaking 4-3 loss to the Phillies in Philadelphia. It was the Cubs' eighth loss in a row. On August 13, the club had a 73-43 record, an 8½-game lead over the second place Cardinals and a 9½-game advantage over the third place Mets. The Mets were in the eighth year of their existence as an NL expansion team and had spent much of the first seven seasons as a universal symbol of failure. Over those seven seasons, the Mets lost 737 games, an average of 105 per year. The Cards quickly fell out of contention while the Mets, a club few, including the Cubs, took seriously surged forward with a 38-11 record from August 14 through the end of the season. Over the same period, the Cubs were 19-27 and finished the season eight games behind the Mets. The devastating fold by the Cubs in 1969 tore the hearts out of fans and everyone connected with the club. The reasons for the collapse are still hot topics for debate in Chicago.

12
September

On this date in 1998 . . .

Sammy Sosa hit his 60th home run of the season during a thrilling 15-12 win over the Brewers at Wrigley Field. Sosa hit the home run in the seventh inning off Valerio de los Santos, and it ended up on the steps of a house on Waveland Avenue. The Brewers led 12-5 in the seventh inning, but the Cubs rebounded to score four runs in the seventh, one in the eighth and five in the ninth for the extraordinary win. The game ended on a three-run, pinch-hit homer by Orlando Merced, whom the Cubs had picked up from the Red Sox only seven days earlier. The next day, Sosa hit his 61st and 62nd home runs of 1998 during a 10-inning, 11-10 win over Milwaukee at Wrigley Field. Sosa became only the second player in major league history to hit at least 62 home runs in a season. The first was Mark McGwire, who reached the figure only five days earlier. The Cubs tied the Brewers 10-10 with two runs in the ninth, one of them on a Sosa homer, and they won the contest on a walk-off home run by Mark Grace with Sosa on deck. After Sosa's second long ball, the crowd's 6½-minute standing ovation delayed the game. Sosa took three curtain calls.

13 September

On this date in 1942 . . .

Cubs shortstop Lennie Merullo tied a major league record by committing four errors in the second inning against the Braves in the second game of a double-header in Boston, Merullo's hometown. Merullo's four errors came in a span of six batters. He fumbled an easy grounder hit by Clyde Kluttz, mishandled a throw from outfielder Bill Nicholson on a single from Ducky Detweiler, bobbled a grounder off the bat of Tommy Holmes and juggled another grounder hit by Skippy Roberge. The Cubs survived Merullo's miscues to win 12-8 in a contest called after eight innings due to a Sunday closing law in Massachusetts stipulating that games must end at 6 p.m. Merullo also made an error in the first game, which the Cubs lost 11-6. He was understandably nervous, because four hours before the start of the first game at a nearby Boston hospital, his wife gave birth to a son that they aptly named "Boots." Formally named Leonard Merullo, Jr., "Boots" later played in the Pittsburgh Pirates organization. His son Matt played in the majors as a catcher, mostly with the White Sox, from 1989 through 1995.

14 September

On this date in 2008 . . .

Carlos Zambrano pitched a no-hitter against the Astros at Miller Park in Milwaukee. The teams played at a neutral site because Hurricane Ike, which struck the Gulf Coast including Houston on September 13, postponed scheduled games between the Cubs and Astros at Minute Maid Park for September 12, 13 and 14. Two of the three games were rescheduled in Milwaukee on September 14 and 15. Zambrano's gem was the first no-hitter by a Cubs pitcher since Milt Pappas threw one on September 2, 1972. Zambrano threw 110 pitches, walked one and struck out 10. He retired the final 13 hitters that he faced. Humberto Quintero grounded out to shortstop Ryan Theriot for the first out of the ninth. Pinch-hitter Jose Castillo was the second out on another weak grounder to Theriot, and Darin Erstad struck out for the final out of the game. The following day, Ted Lilly (seven innings), Jeff Samardzija (one-third of an inning), Carlos Marmol (two-thirds of an inning) and Bob Howry (one inning) combined on a one-hitter to defeat the Astros 6-1 in Milwaukee. The only Houston hit was a single by Mark Loretta with one out in the seventh inning. Zambrano and Lilly pitched 15 consecutive hitless innings.

On this date in 1946 . . .

The second game of a double-header against the Dodgers was called when a swarm of gnats suddenly invaded Ebbets Field in the top of the sixth inning with the Cubs leading 2-0. Dodger hurler Kirby Higbe could not deliver a pitch because he was too busy slapping away at the pesky insects. Umpires claimed that the game was called because of darkness, not because of the gnats, but there was enough daylight to keep playing. The Cubs won the first game 4-3 in 10 innings.

On this date in 1975 . . .

The Pirates crushed the Cubs 22-0 in the most lopsided shutout in modern (since 1900) major league history. The Pirates out hit the Cubs 24-3. Pittsburgh scored nine runs in the first inning and accounted for all 22 runs in the first seven innings off Rick Reuschel, Tom Dettore, Oscar Zamora and Buddy Schultz. Combined with a 9-1 loss to the Pirates the previous day, the Cubs allowed 31 unanswered runs. Rennie Stennett collected seven hits in seven at-bats with a triple, two doubles and four singles. The Cubs held the record for most runs allowed in a shutout loss alone until the Yankees tied it with a 22-0 loss to the Indians on August 31, 2004, in New York.

17
September

On this date in 1953 . . .

Six years after Jackie Robinson's debut, Ernie Banks became the first African American player in Cubs history. Gene Baker actually became the first African American on the Cubs roster when he was called up from the Los Angeles Angels of the Pacific Coast League on August 31. Baker remained in Los Angeles until the PCL season ended on September 13 and made his debut with the Cubs on September 20. The Cubs purchased Banks from the Kansas City Monarchs of the Negro League for $35,000 on September 8. The $35,000 represents the greatest bargain in club history. What Banks means to the Cubs cannot be measured in mere statistics. With his genuinely sunny disposition, optimism and enthusiasm, Banks came to symbolize what was right about baseball and will forever be known as "Mr. Cub."

18
September

On this date in 1999 . . .

Sammy Sosa became the first player in baseball history to hit 60 home runs two seasons in a row, although he could not stop the Cubs from losing 7-4 in 14 innings to the Brewers at Wrigley Field. He hit number 60 off Jason Bere. When Sammy hit number 60, Mark McGwire had 56 on the season. By the end of the year, McGwire hit 65, and Sosa hit 63. At the end of the 2008 season, Sosa had the third highest (66 in 1998), fifth highest (64 in 2001) and sixth highest (63 in 1999) single-season home run totals in major league history. Amazingly, he failed to lead the league in any of those three seasons because Mark McGwire hit 70 in 1998 and 65 in 1999, and Barry Bonds clouted 73 in 2001. Sosa did lead the NL in homers when he hit 50 in 2000 and 49 in 2002.

On this date in 1955 . . .

Ernie Banks became the first player in major league history to hit five grand slams in a season. The record-breaking blast came off the Cardinal's Lindy McDaniel in the seventh inning in St. Louis. The Cards came back to win, however, 6-5 in 12 innings. Banks held the record for most grand slams in a season until Don Mattingly hit six for the Yankees in 1987. Banks still holds the National League record. The five grand slams in 1955 were the first five of Ernie's career. He did not hit another one until 1959. Playing for the Cubs from 1953 through 1971, Banks ranks first among club leaders in games (2,528), first in at-bats (9,421), first in total bases (4,706), second in home runs (512), second in RBIs (1,636), second in hits (2,583), third in doubles (407), fifth in runs (1,305), seventh in triples (90), eighth in slugging percentage (.500) and eighth in walks (763).

The question of the day.

Who was Hank Borowy?

The Cubs purchased Hank Borowy from the Yankees on July 27, 1945, in a transaction that helped Chicago reach the World Series. Larry MacPhail bought the Yankees in April 1945 and took an instant dislike to Borowy, even though he had a 10-5 record on the season at the time he was sold to the Cubs and a 56-30 career mark. MacPhail dismissed Borowy as a "seven-inning pitcher" at a time when pitchers were expected to finish a majority of their starts. With the Cubs, Borowy was 11-2 with a 2.13 ERA over the remainder of the 1945 season. In the process, Borowy became the first of two pitchers to win at least ten games with two teams in the same season. The other was Bartolo Colon with the Indians and Expos in 2002. In the 1945 World Series, Borowy pitched a shutout in game one and four innings of scoreless relief to close out a 12-inning victory in game six. After 1945, however, he had problems with blisters on his fingers and was 25-32 with the Cubs from 1946 through 1948 before he was dealt to the Phillies.

21

September

On this date in 1932 . . .

The Cubs created controversy by letting the players vote on how to divide their World Series shares. Despite managing the club for two-thirds of the season, Rogers Hornsby was ignored completely. He had been fired on August 2 and replaced by Charlie Grimm. Hornsby protested to Kenesaw Landis, but the commissioner refused to intervene. Shortstop Mark Koenig was given only one-half of a share after hitting .353 and playing a key role in the stretch drive for the pennant. The 20 players on the Cubs who drew a full share earned $4,245 for losing the World Series at a time when only the top stars had salaries of $10,000 or more. The division of shares proved to be a source of contention during the World Series. The Yankees continually razzed the Cubs from the dugout over their snubs of Hornsby and former Yankee Koenig. Yankee manager Joe McCarthy, still bitter over being fired by the Cubs two years earlier, further fueled the hatred of the Cubs. The Yankees swept the Cubs to win the Series.

22

September

On this date in 1886 . . .

Near the end of a tight pennant race with the Detroit Wolverines, the Cubs had trouble with Detroit fans. During the 19th century, visiting players dressed at the hotel and traveled to the ballpark in full uniform by carriage. On this day, someone threw a rock into one of the carriages carrying the Cubs and hit a Cubs player. King Kelly and Tom Burns took off after the assailant, and Burns was hit by a man in the crowd. The assemblage closed in on them and "several umbrellas were brandished threateningly." Burns suffered a dislocated thumb during the altercation and missed three weeks. The Cubs won 6-4 in a contest called on account of darkness after six innings. This was quite a contrast to the greeting the Detroit players received in Chicago two months earlier on July 8. West Side Park was decorated, including an arch with the words, "Welcome Detroit." At 3 p.m., a procession arrived, headed by a platoon of Chicago police and followed by the First Regiment Band, carriages carrying the Chicago and Detroit players and 300 fans that traveled from Detroit to root for their Wolverines. The Detroiters marched under the arch to the great cheers of the Windy City fans. The Cubs won the game 9-4.

23
September

On this date in 1908 . . .

The Cubs tied the Giants 1-1 at the Polo Grounds in New York in the most controversial game ever played. The score was 1-1 with two out in the bottom of the ninth with Jack Pfeister pitching for the Cubs. The Giants' Moose McCormick was on third and Fred Merkle was on first. Al Bridwell singled, scoring McCormick. Merkle believed the game was over and headed for the center-field clubhouse without touching second base. Center fielder Solly Hofman threw the ball to second baseman Johnny Evers, but it went over Evers's head and into the crowd, which overran the field. Giants pitcher Joe McGinnity, who was coaching third, retrieved the ball and threw it into the crowd. Cubs pitcher Rube Kroh, who was not in the game, pulled the ball away from a fan and handed it to Evers, who stepped on second for the force out. In the midst of the confusion, base umpire Hank O'Day called Merkle out and ruled the game a 1-1 tie and said play couldn't continue because the crowd had engulfed the field celebrating the Giants "victory." The next day, NL President Harry Pulliam upheld O'Day's decision and declared the game a tie. The contest was replayed on October 8, with the Cubs winning 4-2 to clinch the pennant by one game.

24
September

On this date in 1905 . . .

A frenzied crowd of 26,000 watched the Cubs defeat the Giants 10-5 at West Side Grounds in Chicago. The Cubs scored nine runs in the fifth inning off Joe McGinnity to overcome a 4-0 New York lead. During the wild afternoon, an umpire was injured, and the crowd staged a riot. Umpire Bob Emslie was hit in the chest by a foul tip in the second inning and dropped to the ground as if he had been shot. Players rushed to his side while police fought off the curious mob surging from all directions. A physician was called, and Emslie remained unconscious for 20 minutes. Despite the injury, he insisted on finishing the game. During the delay, the mob that had overflowed the grandstand and the bleachers became unmanageable. Police reinforcements came quickly and made an effort to clear the diamond. According to the wire service reports, "clubs were wielded without mercy, and the air was full with flying headgear. Heads were cracked without compunction and the scene looked like a miniature battlefield."

On this date in 1930 . . .

Joe McCarthy announced his resignation as manager of the Cubs. There were four games left to play. Two days earlier, club owner William Wrigley, Jr. announced that McCarthy would not return in 1931 and would be replaced by Roger Hornsby. Wrigley was 69 years old, in failing health and was desperate to add a world championship baseball team to his legacy. McCarthy came close to a title with the Cubs: in 1927 he had a six-game lead in mid-August but finished in fourth place. In 1928, McCarthy finished only four games behind the first place Cardinals. In 1929, the Cubs won the NL pennant but lost the World Series. And in 1930, McCarthy's Cubs blew a 5½-game lead in two weeks during late-August and early-September. Wrigley died in January 1932 before realizing his dream of winning a world championship. The Yankees named McCarthy their manager on October 10, 1930. He remained on the job until 1946, a period in which he became one of the most successful managers in big-league history. Although William Wrigley, Jr. believed that McCarthy was not a manager who could deliver a world championship team, Joe won eight American League pennants and seven World Series with the Yankees.

On this date in 1979 . . .

Cubs right fielder Larry Biittner lost a ball in his hat during an 8-3 loss to the Mets at Wrigley Field. Biittner raced in to try and catch a sinking line drive by Bruce Boisclair and trapped it. During the chase, Biittner's hat flew off and landed on top of the ball. He ran around in circles looking for the ball before lifting his cap to find it. By this time, Boisclair was streaking toward second. Biittner fired the ball in that direction but overthrew the bag. Bosclair was safe with a double.

27
September

On this date in 1935 . . .

The Cubs clinched the pennant and ran their winning streak to 21 games with 6-2 and 5-3 wins over the Cardinals in St. Louis. The 21-game winning streak is the longest in Cubs history, tying the mark set by the 1880 club. The only longer streak in major league history is the 26-game streak of the 1916 New York Giants. However, the Giants played a tie game between victories number 12 and 13 while winning 26 straight. The 1880 Cubs also had a tie during their 21-game streak. The 1935 Cubs have the longest winning streak in history uninterrupted by a tie game. At the start of the streak on September 4, the Cubs were 2½ games behind the Cardinals and took first place on September 14. Managed by Charlie Grimm, the Cubs won the NL pennant by four games. While winning 21 in a row, the Cubs outscored the opposition 137-53. The pitching staff held opponents to three runs or less in 20 of the 21 games, including four shutouts. The club won two extra-inning games, five by one run and swept two doubleheaders.

28
September

On this date in 1952 . . .

The final day of the season, the Cardinals' Stan Musial made the only pitching appearance of his big-league career during a 3-0 Cubs win over the Cardinals in St. Louis. Musial went into the game with a .336 to .326 lead over Cubs outfielder Frank Baumholtz in the NL batting race. With one out in the first inning, Musial came in from his center-field position to pitch to Baumholtz, while pitcher Harvey Haddix went to center field. A left-handed hitter, Baumholtz switched to the right side and hit a weak grounder to shortstop Solly Hemus, who fumbled the ball for an error. Musial returned to the outfield and won the batting championship, going 1-for-3 while Baumholtz was 1-for-4. Musial finished the year with a .336 average, and Baumholtz ended at .325. Baumholtz was a basketball star at Ohio University, and the school retired his number, 54, in 1995. He played for the Cleveland Rebels in the first year of the NBA from 1946 to 1947 and averaged 14.0 points per game.

On this date in 2004 . . .

Cubs reliever LaTroy Hawkins blew a two-strike, two-out save opportunity for the second time in five days. The Cubs went into the September 25 game against the Mets in New York with 13 wins in their last 16 games and a 1½-game lead over the Giants in the wild-card race. The Cubs led 3-0 with two Mets on base, two out in the ninth and two strikes on rookie Victor Diaz with Hawkins pitching. Diaz hit a three-run home run to tie the score. It was only his second big-league homer. With Kent Mercker on the mound for Chicago, the Mets won the game 4-3 in the 11th inning on the first big-league home run by Craig Brazell. Through 2008, Brazell has yet to homer again in the majors. On September 29, Hawkins was once more one strike away from a save, but the Cubs wound up losing in extra innings. The Cubs led the Reds 2-1 at Wrigley Field with two out in the ninth and no one on base. Hawkins allowed a triple to D'Angelo Jiminez and a two-strike double to Austin Kearns to tie the game. Kearns hit a two-run homer in the 12th off Jon Leicester to lift Cincinnati to a 4-2 lead. The Cubs lost the contest 4-3 and dropped seven of the last nine games to finish three games behind the Astros in the wild-card chase.

On this date in 1920 . . .

Cubs infielder Buck Herzog was stabbed three times following an exhibition game at Joliet, Illinois. Herzog was climbing into his automobile when an individual jumped on the running board and called the Cubs infielder a "crook," a reference to allegations that Herzog helped throw a game on August 31 in collusion with gamblers. Herzog leaped out of his car to fight with the man, and as the two were rolling in the dirt, one of the man's friends stabbed Herzog twice in the hand and once in the calf with a pen knife. Fortunately, Herzog was not seriously injured.

Wrigley Hits 100

October

01
October

On this date in 1932 . . .

Babe Ruth may or may not have "called his shot" during game three of the World Series, won by the Yankees 7-5 over the Cubs before 49,986 fans at Wrigley Field. In the fifth inning, with the score 4-4, Ruth gestured to the Cubs bench and pitcher Charlie Root. He then belted a two-strike pitch from Root into the center-field bleachers for a home run. The meaning of that gesture has been debated for years. There is no reliable film record of the event, and eyewitness testimony varies widely. In their accounts that appeared the following day, some reporters claimed that Ruth pointed to the fence. Some say he held up one finger after the second strike to indicate he still had one pitch left to hit. Others made no mention of any kind of gesture whatsoever. Taking the dozens of accounts of the event into consideration, this is the likeliest scenario: Ruth was responding to razzing from the Cubs bench. Both clubs had been taunting each other unmercifully with what today would be called "trash talking." Ruth pointed his bat at some juncture during the at-bat toward the Cubs bench and toward the outfield, possibly in a sweeping motion. After the second strike, he held up one finger indicating he had one swing left. Then he hit a towering home run.

02
October

On this date in 1984 . . .

The Cubs overwhelmed the Padres 13-0 in the first game of the National League Championship Series before 36,282 spectators in the first postseason game at Wrigley Field since 1945. In 1984, the NLCS was a best-of-five affair, and the next day, the Cubs moved within one victory of the World Series, defeating San Diego 4-2. Following the game, Cubs fan, columnist and ABC commentator George Will said, "We all know that means the Padres in five." Mike Royko took the opposite tack, believing the Cubs were in the World Series after taking two in Chicago. Royko ridiculed San Diego fans in his nationally syndicated column, drawing unflattering comparisons between devoted Cubs followers and laid back Southern Californians. Angered by Royko's rant, Padres fans cheered their club loudly and often, breaking all previous decibel levels at San Diego Stadium. Padres players credited their fans with helping them overcome the two-game deficit to win the playoff series.

On this date in 1915 . . .

The Cubs played their last game at West Side Grounds, which had been their home since 1893. The ballpark held 16,000 in double-decked wooden stands. A balcony of 58 boxes, seating about 600 people, was built atop the grandstand between the bases to accommodate the well-to-do. The structure was ornamented with three green towers and a bandstand on the roof. The left-field fence was 340 feet from home plate, the distance to center a majestic 560 feet and the right-field line extended 316 feet. The clubhouse, which was painted yellow and had a verandah, was located in the deepest part of center field and was in play. The original Comiskey Park opened in 1910, and Weeghman Park, present day Wrigley Field, opened in 1914 for the Chicago Whales of the Federal League. By this time, West Side Grounds was uncomfortable and dilapidated. It was not only one of the worst ballparks in the country, it was only the third best baseball venue in Chicago. In December 1915, the Federal League folded and Charles Weeghman bought the Cubs from a syndicate headed by Charles Murphy. Weeghman moved the Cubs to his ballpark in 1916.

On this date in 1906 . . .

The Cubs won their 116th game of the season with a 4-0 decision over the Pirates in Pittsburgh. The Cubs closed the 1906 season with 55 wins in their last 63 games to finish with a record of 116-36 and set a major league record for wins in a season. The Seattle Mariners tied the record in 2001. They were 116-46 under manager Lou Piniella. The Cubs still hold the modern (since 1900) record for winning percentage in a season at .763. The club started the 1907 campaign 23-4 to give them a regular-season record of 78-12 over two seasons. From April 27, 1906, through August 4, 1907, the Cubs were 181-54 in the regular season, a winning percentage of .770.

On this date in 2003 . . .

The Cubs pulled off an upset in the Division Series by beating the Braves 5-1 in Atlanta in the fifth and deciding game. Kerry Wood pitched eight innings, allowing one run and five hits. Alex Gonzalez put the Cubs ahead 2-0 with a solo homer in the second inning, and Aramis Ramirez made it 4-0 with a two-run shot in the sixth. Joe Borowski closed out the game with a perfect ninth inning, striking out Andruw Jones to end the game. During the regular season, the Braves were 101-61, while the Cubs had a record of 88-74. It was the first postseason series the Cubs won since 1908, ending a streak of ten straight losses. Chicago lost the World Series in 1910, 1918, 1929, 1932, 1935, 1938 and 1945. They were losers in the NLCS in 1984 and 1989 and in the Division Series in 1998. The 2003 Cubs moved on to play the Florida Marlins in the National League Championship Series.

On this date in 1882 . . .

The National League champion Cubs played the American Association champion Cincinnati Reds and lost 4-0 in Cincinnati. The next day, the Cubs turned the tables on the Reds, winning 2-0 in the second game of two postseason exhibitions in the Ohio city. The two contests were the first-ever postseason meetings between teams from rival leagues. The American Association was formed in November 1881 as competition to the established National League, but the two leagues coexisted in a peaceful fashion. NL clubs, like the Cubs, played exhibition games against many AA clubs during spring training and on off days during the regular season. When the regular season ended on October 1, more exhibition games like the ones between the Reds and Cubs were played. The postseason games were not part of a "World Series" to determine a "world champion," however. Only two contests were scheduled. Rumors circulated that AA President Denny McKnight threatened to expel the Reds from the organization if they played the Cubs, but the *Cincinnati Commercial* called the scuttlebutt "the utmost buncombe."

On this date in 1984 . . .

The Cubs lost the fifth and deciding game of the NLCS 6-3 to the Padres in San Diego. The winning pitcher was Craig Lefferts, who held the Cubs hitless in the sixth and seventh. The Cubs traded Lefferts to the Padres on December 7, 1983. The loss left everyone connected with the Cubs crushed and dumbfounded. Through the first 22 innings of the series, the Cubs outscored the Padres 18-2, were 12 outs from the World Series with a three-run lead and were eight outs away with a one-run advantage. A World Series in Chicago seemed to be in the bag. "We had them by the throat and let them get away," said general manager Dallas Green.

On this date in 1907 . . .

The World Series between the Cubs and Tigers opened before 24,377 at West Side Grounds in Chicago and ended after 12 innings because of darkness in a 3-3 tie. The Cubs trailed 3-1 before rallying with two runs in the ninth. Frank Chance led off with a single, and Harry Steinfeldt was hit by a pitch. Johnny Kling popped out, but Johnny Evers reached on an error to load the bases. Wildfire Schulte was retired on a grounder with Frank Chance scoring to make it 3-2. The other two runners moved up a base. Del Howard pinch-hit for Joe Tinker and swung and missed at a two-strike pitch on a low curveball for what should have been the final out, but the Cubs caught a huge break when the ball got past Tiger catcher Boss Schmidt, allowing Steinfeldt to score from third base. The inning ended when Evers was out trying to steal home. Curiously, the two teams wore the same color uniforms while scoring the same number of runs. After losing three games at home during the 1906 World Series, the Cubs believed their home whites were a jinx and donned their gray road uniforms for game one.

09 October

On this date in 1906 . . .

The Cubs and the White Sox met in the first game of an all-Chicago World Series. Amid snow flurries, the White Sox defeated the Cubs 2-1 before 12,693 at West Side Grounds. The Cubs came into the Series with momentum, compiling a 116-36 regular-season record after winning 55 of their last 63 games. By contrast, the 1906 White Sox were 93-58 and known as the "Hitless Wonders" because they won a pennant with a .230 team batting average and only seven home runs. In addition, the Sox were in only the sixth season of their existence. By contrast, the Cubs had been around since 1876. The confrontation appeared to be a mismatch, and the Cubs were heavy betting favorites at 3-1. Chicago was at a virtual standstill for the six days in which the two clubs battled for the world title. The 1906 World Series was marked by great pitching performances, bitterly cold weather and one of the biggest upsets in the history of the Fall Classic. In the end, the White Sox won the World Series four games to two. Cubs player-manager Frank Chance vowed the Cubs would return to the World Series to win. The promise was fulfilled when the Cubs won the world championship in 1907 and 1908, both times over Detroit.

10 October

On this date in 1945 . . .

The Cubs lost the seventh and deciding game of the World Series 9-3 to the Detroit Tigers before 41,590 at Wrigley Field. Manager Charlie Grimm gambled by bringing back Hank Borowy as the starting pitcher, despite his five innings as a starter in game five and a four-inning relief stint in game six two days earlier. Borowy failed to retire a batter as the Tigers scored five runs in the first inning. It was the seventh World Series loss in a row for the Cubs, following failures in 1910, 1918, 1929, 1932, 1935 and 1938.

On this date in 2003 . . .

The Cubs came within one victory of the World Series with an 8-3 NLCS game-four win over the Marlins in Miami. Aramis Ramirez paced the attack with two homers, a single and six RBIs. The first homer by Ramirez was a grand slam off Dontrelle Willis in the first inning after Willis walked the bases loaded. The Cubs put the game away early with a 7-0 lead after three innings. The winning pitcher was Matt Clement. All the Cubs had to do to reach the Fall Classic for the first time since 1945 was to win one of three games against the Marlins, including two at Wrigley Field, but the curse prevailed as the Cubs dropped all of the next three games.

On this date in 1907 . . .

The Cubs won their first World Series by defeating the Tigers 2-0 in game five before only 7,370 on a cold and snowy afternoon in Detroit. The first game of the series ended in a tie before the Cubs won the next four. Mordecai Brown wrapped up the title with a five-hit shutout. Harry Steinfeldt had three hits, including an RBI-single in the first to give the Cubs a 1-0 lead, and a triple. The Cubs stole 18 bases in the five-game series, which still stands as the record in the Fall Classic. Chicago pitchers allowed only six runs, four of them earned. The Cubs and the Tigers met again in 1908, with the Cubs again winning four games to one. The deciding game-five victory happened on October 14 with the Cubs winning 2-0 in Detroit behind Orval Overall's three-hit shutout. He struck out 10, four of them in the first inning. The four-strikeout inning was possible because Claude Rossman swung and missed at a two-strike pitch but reached safely when the ball sailed past catcher Johnny Kling. The attendance was only 6,210, the smallest in Series history. It was also the shortest by time in World Series history, lasting only one hour and 25 minutes.

13 October

The question of the day.

What is the only team in World Series history to blow an eight-run lead?

The Cubs led the Athletics in game four on October 12, 1929, in Philadelphia, but the A's scored 10 runs in the eighth inning to win 10-8. Misplays from center fielder Hack Wilson, who lost two balls in the sun, one for an inside-the-park home run by Mule Haas that scored three runs, helped Philadelphia. Six of the runs were scored off Charlie Root, two off Art Nehf (in his last major league appearance) and two against Sheriff Blake. The Cubs also blew what seemed like a certain victory the following day in game five. Pat Malone took a 2-0 lead into the bottom of the ninth but allowed three runs to lose the game 3-2, and the Cubs lost the Series four games to one.

14 October

On this date in 2003 . . .

In game six of the NLCS, the Marlins scored eight runs in the eighth inning to defeat the Cubs 8-3 at Wrigley Field. Chicago took a 3-0 lead with single runs in the first, sixth and seventh innings. After Mark Mordecai flied out to start the eighth inning, the Cubs were just five outs away from the World Series. With a three-run lead, no one on base and Mark Prior on the mound, the Cubs were in good shape. Since August 4, Prior had been 12-1 with a 1.44 ERA, including the postseason. Juan Pierre started the Florida rally with a double. Luis Castillo, the next batter, hit a foul ball toward the left-field stands where Bartman deflected it away from Moises Alou. Alou slammed his glove in anger, believing that could have been the second out. Whether Alou would have caught the ball is questionable, but even so, the Cubs still had a 3-0 lead with one out in the eighth. Castillo wound up on first with a walk. Two batters later with the Cubs still ahead 3-1, shortstop Alex Gonzalez booted a potential inning-ending double play grounder. When the inning was over, the Marlins had sent 12 batters to the plate and scored eight runs, five of them off Prior.

On this date in 2003 . . .

The Cubs lost an opportunity to reach the World Series with a 9-6 loss to the Marlins in game seven at Wrigley Field. Florida scored three runs in the first inning on a homer by Miguel Cabrera off Kerry Wood, but the Cubs countered with three in their half, the last two on Wood's homer. Moises Alou put the Cubs up 5-3 with a two-run bomb in the third. The Marlins zeroed in on Wood, however, scoring three runs in the fifth and one in the sixth, then adding two in the seventh off Kyle Farnsworth. The last run of the contest came on a Troy O'Leary pinch-hit home run in the seventh. It was Chicago's only hit during the last six innings. The Marlins went on to defeat the Yankees four games to two in the World Series.

The question of the day.

Who was Howard Ehmke?

Howard Ehmke was the surprise starter for the Philadelphia Athletics in game one of the 1929 World Series, played before 50,740 at Wrigley Field on October 8. He went on to beat the Cubs 3-1 with an eight-hitter and 13 strikeouts. A's manager Connie Mack bypassed 24-game winner George Earnshaw and 20-game winner, future Hall of Famer Lefty Grove to use Ehmke, a journeyman who pitched only 54⅔ innings during the regular season, with a 7-2 record and only 15 strikeouts. Mack believed that Ehmke's assortment of breaking balls would neutralize the Cubs, especially with the center-field bleachers full with white-shirted spectators. Ehmke's big-league career ended the following season, and he never won another game.

17
October

On this date in 1953 . . .

P. K. Wrigley appointed Bill Veeck as a special advisor "to spearhead the campaign to bring major league baseball to Los Angeles." Veeck sold the St. Louis Browns three weeks earlier to a group that moved the franchise to Baltimore, where they were renamed the Orioles. At the time, Wrigley owned the Los Angeles Angels minor league club in the Pacific Coast League. In 1953, big-league owners were debating over whether to expand the two eight-team leagues to 10 teams, with Los Angeles as one of the expansion franchises, or to create a third major league with eight teams located west of the Mississippi River. "Bill will not only help Los Angeles get a major league club," said Wrigley, "his job also is to go out and organize the effort so that Los Angeles and possibly other Pacific Coast League cities get top-flight baseball in an orderly and sensible way as soon as it becomes physically possible." Veeck remained with the Cubs until 1955 when L.A.'s fate as a major league city still had not been decided. Wrigley sold the Angels to Dodgers owner Walter O'Malley in February 1957. O'Malley moved his franchise from Brooklyn to Los Angeles the following October. On March 10, 1959, Veeck purchased a controlling interest in the White Sox.

18
October

The question of the day.

Who was James Ridner?

James Ridner is proof that it does not pay to bet on the Cubs to win. He had to push a baby carriage from Kentucky to Michigan because he wagered that the Cubs would defeat the Tigers in the 1935 World Series. To settle the bet, Ridner pushed the carriage from his home in Harlan, Kentucky, to Detroit. Inside the carriage was Arson "Fireball" Stephens, the winner of the wager, along with provisions for the journey. The 550-mile trip took 30 days to complete and ended at home plate at Tiger Stadium. Ridner wore out two baby carriages and three pairs of shoes.

Happy Birthday Bob O'Farrell.

Bob O'Farrell was born on this date in 1896. He was a catcher for the Cubs from 1915 through 1925 and again in 1934 during a 21-year major league career. He was injured in a bizarre manner on July 23, 1924, when he suffered a fractured skull during a 3-1 loss to the Braves in Chicago. Absent-mindedness and borrowed equipment contributed to the injury. The clubhouse boy forgot to bring the catcher's mask that O'Farrell used on a regular basis. O'Farrell sent back for it but did not want to hold up the game, so he put on an old mask that did not fit him properly, just to catch the inning. Stuffy McInnis hit a foul tip that struck O'Farrell's mask and drove it into his forehead, causing the fracture above the right eye. It was that kind of year for the Cubs. Left fielder Denver Grigsby suffered facial injuries twice in August. First, he lost a fly ball in the sun and was struck in the face, breaking his sunglasses. Then, he ran face-first into the screen in front of the bleachers at Wrigley Field and received an assortment of cuts and abrasions.

The question of the day.

Who is the only player to be picked off twice in a World Series game?

Cubs outfielder Max Flack had an embarrassing afternoon in game four of the 1918 World Series, a 3-2 loss to the Red Sox, on September 9 at Fenway Park. Flack led off the game with a single but was picked off when catcher Sam Agnew threw to first baseman Stuffy McInnis for the putout. Flack was nailed again in the fourth inning while on second base when Red Sox pitcher Babe Ruth wheeled and fired to shortstop Everett Scott. Two days later in Boston, Flack helped lose game six in the field. With two out in the third inning and runners on second and third, Flack dropped a liner off the bat of George Whitehead, allowing both runners to score. The two runs held up for a 2-1 victory, which gave the Red Sox their last world championship until 2004.

21
October

On this date in 1910 . . .

Cubs pitcher Orval Overall announced his retirement. Since being acquired by the Cubs in a trade with the Reds in 1906, Overall had a record of 82-38 with the club and pitched in four World Series. "I am just tired of the job," said Overall, "and I don't want any more of it. The life of a big-league pitcher is unsatisfactory at best. If you are good, you get along all right and nobody has a complaint. But if you are bad, even for a little while, or your arm backs up on you, you are up against it and can't help yourself." Overall returned to the Cubs in 1913, but was 4-5 in 11 games and retired for good.

22
October

On this date in 1974 . . .

Longtime Wrigley Field announcer Pat Pieper died at the age of 88. The Cubs had employed Pieper since 1904, starting as a vendor at West Side Grounds. In 1916, when the club moved to present day Wrigley Field, Pieper was hired as the field announcer, carrying a 14-pound megaphone and walking up and down in front of the stands to shout the starting lineups. In 1932, an electric public address system was installed, and Pieper was provided with a spot almost directly behind home plate. Wearing his trademark brown suit, he launched every game by saying, "Attention, Attention, please! Have your pencils and scorecards ready, and I will give the correct lineups for today's game." When he was still in his 80s, Pieper moonlighted as a waiter at the Ivanhoe Restaurant 12 blocks south of Wrigley Field, where he worked immediately after the game was over. Pieper provided one memorable moment when several fans in the bleachers draped their coats over the outfield wall. Pieper turned on his microphone and announced to the crowd, "Will the bleachers fans please remove their clothing?"

The question of the day.

Who threw the only one-hitter for the Cubs in a World Series game?

There has been one no-hitter and four nine-inning, complete-game one-hitters in World Series history. Claude Passeau of the Cubs threw one of the one-hitters on October 5, 1945, in game three, defeating the Tigers 3-0 in Detroit. The only two Tigers to reach base were Rudy York on a second-inning single and Bob Swift on a sixth-inning walk. Passeau pitched for the Cubs from 1939 through 1947 and won 124 games. He is probably best remembered, though, for an ignominious moment during the 1941 All-Star Game in Detroit. Passeau came in late in the game as a reliever and surrendered a three-run, ninth-inning walk-off home run to Ted Williams, blowing the win for the NL, which lost 7-5. Passeau also is still in the record books for the most consecutive chances accepted by a pitcher without an error with 273 from May 21, 1941, through May 20, 1946. He achieved the record despite wearing the smallest glove in the majors. The small glove was necessary because of a childhood accident that left two fingers of his left hand permanently bent down and almost useless. While riding in the back of a pick-up truck, the shotgun he was holding went off and the bullet passed through his right hand and went out his wrist.

Happy Birthday Jim Brosnan.

Born on this date in 1929, Jim Brosnan was a Cubs pitcher from 1954 through 1958 who also became a best-selling author. While pitching for the Cardinals and Reds in 1959, he wrote an autobiographical diary of the campaign called *The Long Season*. Still in Cincinnati, Brosnan followed with a similar book about the 1961 season titled *The Pennant Race*. The books were the first of the diary genre that presented an inside look at Major League Baseball from a player's perspective. Brosnan was also one of three Cubs pitchers who combined to set a major league record by walking nine batters in one inning during a 9-5 loss to the Reds in Cincinnati on April 24, 1957. Moe Drabowsky was on the mound at the start of the walkathon. After retiring the first batter, Drabowsky walked four in a row. Jackie Collum relieved, faced five batters and walked three. Brosnan replaced Collum and walked two more. The Reds recorded only one hit in the inning, a single by George Crowe off Collum but scored seven runs.

On this date in 1965 . . .

Cubs owner P. K. Wrigley shocked the baseball world by hiring fiery, blunt and outspoken 60-year-old Leo Durocher as manager of the long-moribund Cubs. At that point, the club had not finished in the top half of the National League standings since 1946. Durocher signed a three-year contract that brought hope and excitement to the Cubs nation. At the time of his arrival, Durocher had not managed a team in more than 10 years, but he was already a legend and one of the most controversial figures in baseball, as well as a national celebrity. He managed the Dodgers from 1939 until 1946 and again in 1948, and the Giants from 1948 through 1955, winning National League pennants in 1941 and 1951. With Durocher at the helm, the Cubs sank into last place in 1966 with a 59-103 record, but things turned around with five consecutive winning seasons from 1967 through 1971. He was fired in July 1972 when he aroused considerable antagonism among his players with his ruthless and insatiable desire to win and his lack of diplomacy or tact.

The question of the day.

What would have happened if the 1918 World Series between the Cubs and the Red Sox had been played in October?

It is only speculative, but if the 1918 Series had been played in October, it might have been canceled by a flu epidemic. The Series that season was originally scheduled for October, like all of the others, but in July of that year, with the country engaged in World War I, the federal government issued an order requiring all men of draft age to enlist in the military or find a war-related job. Baseball's regular season ended on September 2, and the World Series was played from September 5 through September 11. From late-September through early-November, a virulent form of influenza struck the nation. Estimates are that 20 to 25 percent of the nation's population was struck by the flu. Health officials banned public gatherings in many cities, including Chicago and Boston, during October and November. The epidemic caused between 400,000 and 500,000 deaths nationwide and 50 million worldwide.

The question of the day.

Who was Charlie Pick?

Cubs outfielder Charlie Pick ended game three of the 1918 World Series, played on September 7 in Chicago, with an ill-advised attempt to score on a passed ball. The Red Sox led 2-1 with two out in the bottom of the ninth when Pick beat out an infield hit and stole second. With Turner Barber batting, Boston hurler Carl Mays shot a pitch past catcher Wally Schang that rolled 20 feet behind the plate. Pick darted for third. Schang made a quick recovery but threw high to third baseman Fred Thomas, who got a glove on the ball and knocked it a few feet into foul territory. Pick tried for home, but was out on a perfect throw from Thomas to Schang.

Happy Birthday Ralph Kiner.

An outfielder with the Cubs in 1953 and 1954 and a future Hall of Famer, Ralph Kiner was born on this date in 1922. On June 4, 1953, the Cubs sent six players to the Pirates along with $150,000 to obtain Kiner and three other players. Kiner led the NL in home runs seven consecutive seasons, from 1946 through 1952. In 971 at-bats with the Cubs over two seasons, he batted .284 with 50 home runs, but those numbers had declined from the batting marks he put up in Pittsburgh. Not to mention whatever Kiner gave the Cubs offensively, he took away on defense. With a bad back hampering his mobility, Kiner was capable of playing only left field, and the Cubs already had a slow-footed power hitter in left in Hank Sauer, who tied Kiner for the home run leadership in 1952. Sauer moved to right field, where he did not have the arm for the position, and Frank Baumholtz moved from right to center, where he did not possess the speed to cover the vast territory between two corner outfielders who could barely move. Kiner got a lot of mileage during his long broadcasting career by joking about how he and Sauer yelled, "You take it, Frankie" to Baumholtz every time a fly ball was hit into the outfield. But it was no laughing matter to Cubs pitchers who watched easy fly balls drop for extra-base hits.

On this date in 1987 . . .

Dallas Green resigned, ending his controversial six-year reign as general manager. He was hired on October 15, 1981, after leading the Phillies to the 1980 world championship as field manager. The Cubs were 38-65 in the strike-shortened 1981 season and had not had a winning year since 1972. Autocratic, heavy-handed and impetuous with a nasty temperament, Green wasted no time in putting his stamp on the Cubs, adopting a slogan, "Building a New Tradition." He immediately launched a campaign to get lights installed at Wrigley Field. Green remade the Cubs with a series of controversial trades that turned a spiritless, talent-depleted team into a division winner in 1984. The division title was followed by three more losing seasons, however, and Green had most of his authority taken away by the Tribune Company. He left the organization well stocked with talent through the excellent scouting staff he assembled, however. When Green submitted his resignation, the Cubs had a long list of players who were productive for many more seasons after 1987. Green's successors blew a golden opportunity to build the Cubs into a consistent pennant-winner.

Happy Birthday Ed Delahanty.

Born on this date in 1867, Delahanty was an outfielder with the Phillies when he became the first player in major league history to hit four home runs in a game on July 13, 1896, in Chicago. The Cubs survived the onslaught to win 9-8. All four homers were hit off Adonis Terry. Delahanty also had a single and drove in seven runs. One homer was hit into the left-field bleachers, one cleared the right-field wall and two were inside-the-park. Both inside-the-park homers were hit over the head of center fielder Bill Lange. One of them bounced behind the clubhouse, which was in play about 500 feet from home plate. The Cubs fans applauded Delahanty wildly for his efforts, and the cheering did not stop until he stepped onto the team omnibus to leave for the hotel.

31
October

The question of the day.

How did a New York City blackout affect the Cubs?

A blackout of electrical power in New York struck during a game between the Cubs and Mets at Shea Stadium on July 13, 1977. The lights went out at 9:31 p.m., with Lenny Randle at bat for the Mets and the Cubs leading 2-1 in the bottom of the sixth. An auxiliary generator kept the public address system and some of the lights in the seating areas operating, but it was not powerful enough to keep the field lights turned on. The game was suspended at 10:52 p.m. with the intention of completing it before the regularly scheduled contest the next evening. The Cubs showered and dressed in a dark locker room and went back to the Waldorf-Astoria Hotel. With the elevators out, the players had to take the stairs holding candles to their rooms, some as high as the 17th floor. The next day, the Cubs took their luggage back down the stairs, went to Shea Stadium and dressed again in the dark, only to be told that the suspended and regularly scheduled games were called off because power was not yet restored. The Cubs took a bus to Philadelphia, where they played a double-header on July 15. The suspended game was finished on September 16 with the Cubs winning 5-2.

Wrigley Hits 100

November

01
November

The question of the day.

When did the Cubs go 48 innings without scoring a run?

The Cubs failed to score in 48 straight innings from June 15 through June 21, 1968. The streak tied a major league set by the 1906 Philadelphia Athletics. It started when the Cubs failed to score in the last eight innings of a 10-inning, 3-2 loss to the Braves in Atlanta on June 15. A day later, the Cubs dropped a 1-0 decision to the Braves in 11 innings at Atlanta-Fulton County Stadium. From June 18 through June 20, the Cardinals swept the Cubs by scores of 1-0, 4-0 and 1-0. On June 21, the Cubs finally scored in the third inning of a 3-2 win over the Reds in Cincinnati. The run-less streak was broken when Reds pitcher George Culver walked the bases loaded and Billy Williams hit a sacrifice fly. Over the course of the 48-inning streak, the Cubs collected 30 hits, left 31 men on base and allowed 10 runs.

02
November

The question of the day.

What were the worst weather conditions for a Cubs game in the history of Wrigley Field?

The Cubs beat snow, rain, bitterly cold weather and the Dodgers to win 9-4 on April 4, 1996, a day unfit for man or beast, much less baseball. The number of tickets sold was 12,626, but only a few thousand brave souls showed up for the game. The temperature was 34 degrees when the first pitch was thrown with a 19-mile-per-hour northerly gale that dropped the wind chill to 12 above zero. The aisles in the ballpark had to be salted to keep people from slipping.

03 November

The question of the day.

Who named their son Wrigley Fields?

On September 12, 2007, Paul and Teri Fields of Michigan City, Indiana, celebrated the birth of their son by naming him Wrigley Alexander Fields. His parents said the child could go by his middle name when he was old enough to decide, but for now, he would be Wrigley Fields. David Ogrin, a golfer on the PGA tour and a diehard Cubs fan from Waukegan, Illinois, named his son Clark Addison after the two streets that intersect outside of the main entrance at Wrigley Field.

04 November

On this date in 1888 . . .

The All-Americans defeated the Cubs 14-4 in San Francisco before a crowd of 10,000. The game was part of a worldwide tour in which the Cubs played a team of All-Stars from clubs in the National League and American Association during the 1888–1889 off-season. The Cubs visited the White House on October 8 to meet with President Grover Cleveland. The tour began in Chicago, and travelled west with contests in Minnesota, Iowa, Nebraska, Colorado, Utah and California. Before the tour ended in March 1889, games were played in Hawaii, New Zealand, Australia, Ceylon, India, Egypt, Italy, France, England and Ireland. On February 9, in what can be described as the ultimate sandlot game, the All-Americans defeated the Cubs 10-6 in the shadow of the Pyramids outside Cairo, Egypt. On February 22, King Humbert of Italy was in the audience at the Villa Borghesi outside Rome. On March 12, the Cubs played at the Surrey County Cricket Club in Kensington Oval in London in the presence of the Prince of Wales. The final game was played in Dublin on March 27. On April 15, the Cubs and the All-Americans were invited to the White House to meet with new President Benjamin Harrison.

05
November

The question of the day.

Why did Frank Chance intentionally miss pop-ups in his major league debut?

Frank Chance made his major league debut as a catcher on April 29, 1898, in a 16-2 win over Louisville in the home opener at West Side Grounds. The pitcher was Clark Griffith, who had an unusual superstition. Griffith believed that shutouts were bad luck. If he had not allowed a run before the ninth inning, he would intentionally groove pitches or walk batters so that the opposition would score. From 1891 through 1897, Griffith made 167 major league starts, completed 127 of them and had a lifetime record of 106-68 with only one shutout. That was a 2-0 victory over the Reds in 1897 when he had little margin for error. During the April 29 contest in 1898, Griffith ordered Chance to miss two pop-ups that dropped harmlessly to the ground and allowed Louisville to plate two runs in the ninth. Griffith eventually decided that shutouts were not a curse after all and pitched a total of 22 of them before his career ended in 1914. He led the league in shutouts in both 1900 and 1901.

06
November

The question of the day.

How did Julio Zuleta "help" break an eight-game losing streak in 2001?

A reserve first baseman, Julio Zuleta decided something drastic needed to be done to break the losing streak. Inspired by the voodoo-practicing Pedro Cerrano from the 1989 film *Major League* and its two sequels, Zuleta took the Cubs bats and struck them handle first through the dugout fencing before a May 20 game against the Diamondbacks in Phoenix. He lit a fire under them, rubbed discarded chicken bones on them, waved fruit under them and chanted to them. Unlike Cerrano in the film, Zuleta stopped short of cutting the heads off chickens. Nonetheless, the spell worked as the Cubs defeated the Diamondbacks 6-2. The victory launched a 12-game winning streak.

07
November

On this date in 1928 . . .

The Cubs sent Socks Seybold, Percy Jones, Lou Legett, Freddy Maguire, Bruce Cunningham and $200,000 to the Boston Braves for Rogers Hornsby. Braves owner Judge Emil Fuchs was in debt and needed the cash to keep his franchise solvent. The Cubs had record attendance figures in 1927 and 1928, but they had just missed winning the pennant, in part because of a weakness at second base. One of the best second baseman in baseball history, Hornsby was seen as the last piece of the puzzle the Cubs needed. At the time of the trade, Hornsby was 32 years old and had a .361 lifetime batting average, .575 slugging percentage, 2,475 hits and 238 home runs. He led the National League in batting average (.387), on-base percentage (.498) and slugging percentage (.632). In Chicago in 1929, Hornsby had one of the greatest offensive years in Cubs history and the club won the NL pennant. He batted .380 and led the league in runs (156) and slugging percentage (.679), in addition to hitting 39 homers, 47 doubles and 229 hits. Beginning in 1930, however, Rogers was hampered by a series of injuries, and his playing time and abilities diminished. From September 1930 through August 1932, Hornsby was also manager of the team.

08
November

On this date in 1912 . . .

Cupid Childs, who played for the Cubs in 1900 and 1901, died at the age of 45. One of the top second baseman of the 1890s, Childs was at the end of his career when he played in Chicago. He was involved in a memorable incident on May 6, 1900, following a 7-6 win over the Pirates at West Side Grounds when he fought Pittsburgh player-manager Fred Clarke in a train station. The two had nearly came to blows during the game when Clarke slid hard into Childs, trying to break up a double play. Cupid went looking for Clarke while the two clubs were waiting for a train to Pittsburgh and cold-cocked Clarke, fueling an all-out brawl. There was no attempt to break up the battle, as a ring was formed with players on each club urging on their teammate. Childs and Clarke pummeled each other with a vengeance. Clarke's face was bloodied, but he left several marks on Childs and tore the shirt almost completely off the Cubs infielder. Policemen broke up the fight. Many Cubs were so disgusted with Childs' behavior that they were rooting for Clarke to win the fight. "Childs made a fool of himself," said outfielder Jimmy Ryan, "and is entitled to no sympathy."

09
November

On this date in 1925 . . .

The Cubs sold shortstop Rabbit Maranville to the Dodgers. The Cubs had acquired him in October 1924 from the Phillies. With the Cubs holding a 33-42 record on July 6, 1925, they appointed Maranville as player-manager, replacing Bill Killefer. The fun-loving but quick-tempered Maranville was hired despite his propensity for pranks and alcohol, and he was clearly the wrong choice to lead a losing club. The fact was made abundantly clear within 24 hours of his appointment. Rabbit celebrated his promotion by getting drunk, then poured ice water all over his players sleeping on the train. Once the Cubs arrived in New York, Maranville got into an altercation with a cab driver and the police. He shared the taxi with infielder Pinky Pittenger and pitcher Herb Brett. When the trio exited the vehicle, the driver mumbled something about a lack of a tip. Maranville was threatening to punch the driver's lights out when police intervened. The new Cubs manager fought with two officers before being subdued and was taken to the station house along with Pittenger and Brett. His title as manager was taken away on September 3.

10
November

On this date in 1992 . . .

Chuck Connors, a first baseman with the Cubs in 1951, died. Connors played only 67 games in the majors, 66 of them with the Cubs, and hit only .238 with two homers, but he had a long and fascinating life. Before reaching the big leagues in baseball, Connors played for the Boston Celtics from 1946 through 1948. Prior to the first game in Boston Celtics history on November 5, 1946, the six foot five Connors shattered the glass backboard in pre-game warm-ups, delaying the contest for a half-hour. While playing in Los Angeles in the Cubs minor league system, he caught the attention of a Hollywood producer and went into acting. Chuck's film debut was in 1952 in the Spencer Tracy-Katherine Hepburn vehicle *Pat and Mike*. Connors was Luke McCain, the lead character on the popular television series *The Rifleman* from 1957 through 1962. He appeared in numerous movies and television dramas until his death and won critical acclaim in the role of a slave owner in the 1977 mini-series *Roots*.

11
November

The question of the day.

In what game did eight Cubs pitchers combine to no-hit the opposition for 12⅔ consecutive innings?

Eight Cubs pitchers combined for 12⅓ straight hitless innings on July 6, 1980, but the club wound up losing 5-4 in 20 innings to the Pirates at Three Rivers Stadium. Pittsburgh led 4-2 before Bill Buckner homered in the eighth, and Cliff Johnson followed with another homer in the ninth on a 2-2 pitch with two out. The pitchers who contributed to the hitless streak were Rick Reuschel (one-third of an inning with the last out of the sixth), George Riley (two innings), Bruce Sutter (two innings), Doug Capilla (one-third of an inning), Dick Tidrow (one-third of an inning), Willie Hernandez (2⅓ innings), Bill Caudill (five innings) and Dennis Lamp (one-third of an inning before Lee Lacy singled with one out in the 19th). During the streak, Chicago pitchers walked eight batters and struck out 13. There were 10 consecutive scoreless innings by both pitching staffs before Omar Moreno singled in the winning run off Lamp in the 20th. The Cubs used 23 of their 24 available players.

12
November

The question of the day.

When were 15 home runs hit in a double-header at Wrigley Field?

The Cubs and the Milwaukee Braves combined to set a major league record for most home runs in a double-header with 15 on May 30, 1956. The Braves hit nine homers and the Cubs clubbed six. In the first game, won 10-9 by the Cubs, there were nine home runs. Bobby Thomson hit two for Milwaukee, while Eddie Mathews, Hank Aaron and Joe Adcock added one each. Gene Baker, Turk Lown, Hobie Landrith and Dee Fondy went deep for Chicago. The homer by Lown was the only one he hit in 214 at-bats in 11 seasons. In the second contest, with the Braves winning 11-9, there were six more homers, four by Milwaukee. Thomson hit two more, giving him four round-trippers on the day, and Mathews and Aaron also went long again. Cubs homers were by Ernie Banks and Harry Chiti. There was also a fight to enliven the afternoon. In the first inning of the first game, Mathews, Aaron and Thomson hit back-to-back-to-back homers off Russ Meyer. The next hitter was Bill Bruton, who Meyer plunked with a pitch. Bruton rushed to the mound, and he and Meyer exchanged punches. Both were ejected.

13
November

The question of the day.

What speed record did the Cubs set in 1911?

Carrying the Cubs from St. Louis on May 29, 1911, the Pennsylvania Railroad set a speed record, covering the 191 miles from Columbus to Pittsburgh in 215 minutes and breaking the old mark by five minutes. The train moved quickly to ensure the Cubs would reach Pittsburgh in time for a game against the Pirates. The train lurched back and forth on the white-knuckle ride. According to the 1912 *Reach Guide,* "it was like walking the quarter-deck of a lake steamer in a cyclone to go the length of the car." In the dining car, Cubs trainer Doc Semmons was munching on some roast beef when he was pitched out of his seat, and while he was lying on the floor, his drink, silverware, plate and the remainder of his dinner, fell on top of him. The Cubs made it to Pittsburgh on time to defeat the Pirates 4-1.

14
November

The question of the day.

What American Indian was the target of Cubs fans in 1898?

The Cubs lost 11-2 and won 4-3 against the Cleveland Spiders in a raucous, separate-admission double-header in Chicago on July 4, 1898. About 12,000 attended the second game, some 500 equipped with firecrackers and revolvers in celebration of the Fourth of July and a military victory the previous day during the Spanish-American War when Theodore Roosevelt and his forces stormed San Juan Hill. When a great play was made, the armed rooters flashed their guns and shot live ammunition into the air. Cleveland right fielder Louis Sockalexis, a Native American, was the target for many of the firecrackers and stood a big part of the game in a blue haze. On July 4, 1900, approximately 1,000 fans appeared at West Side Grounds armed with revolvers and pistols and fired them constantly in celebration of the holiday during a double-header against the Phillies.

On this date in 1983 . . .

Charlie Grimm died at the age of 85. He was associated with the Cubs for nearly 60 years. Grimm was known as "Jolly Cholly" for his light-hearted nature. He played for the Cubs from 1925 through 1936 and spent three different terms as manager (1932–1938, 1944–1949 and 1960). Grimm played for the Cubs in two World Series as a first baseman and managed the club in three (1932, 1935 and 1945). He was also a coach, scout, consultant, vice president and broadcaster with the club. In accordance with Charlie's wishes, his wife Marion scattered his ashes over Wrigley Field in April 1984.

Happy Birthday Clay Bryant.

A pitcher with the Cubs from 1935 through 1940, Clay Bryant was born on this date in 1911. He entered the 1938 season as a 26-year-old with only 11 big-league victories. But he came out of nowhere to post a 19-11 record in the 1938 pennant chase with a 3.10 ERA in 270⅓ innings. After 1938, arm injuries ended Bryant's effectiveness. He pitched only two more seasons and had a 2-2 record and a 5.31 ERA in 57⅔ innings. On June 4, 1940, the Cubs suspended Bryant indefinitely without pay because he was unable to pitch with a sore elbow. Bryant wanted to go to Los Angeles to seek treatment for his arm, but he could not afford the trip and the medical bills without a steady paycheck. He appealed the suspension to Kenesaw Landis, but the commissioner told the pitcher that the club was well within its rights to suspend him. P. K. Wrigley would not budge and refused to lift the suspension or pay for Bryant's treatment, but Wrigley did come up with a unique way to help him. Wrigley hired Bryant's wife Opal at $50 per week for four weeks. Mrs. Bryant's "job" was to accompany her husband to Los Angeles and make certain he received proper attention for his ailing wing. Bryant never pitched another big-league game after 1940.

November 17

On this date in 1877 . . .

The Cubs secured a lease to build a new ballpark at the southeast corner of Michigan Avenue and Randolph Street. It was on the same site as a previous ballpark that was destroyed in the Great Chicago Fire in 1871. The new facility was called Lakefront Park. Right field extended southward along Michigan Avenue to a point midway between Washington and Madison Streets. The left-field fence paralleled Randolph Street. To the east, toward Lake Michigan, lay the yards of the Illinois Central Railroad. The lake itself was just beyond the tracks. Landfills in later years pushed the lakefront eastward. The new park began with a seating capacity of 3,000. The infield was bumpy and littered with rocks, boulders, ashes, glasses and bottles because the land previously served as a dumping ground for the debris left over from the 1871 fire. The outfield was probably the smallest in major league history. The fences were so close that any ball hit over them was a ground rule double. The wind off the lake made attending a game an unpleasant experience because of swirling dust from the infield and the nearby unpaved streets and sandy beaches.

November 18

On this date in 1971 . . .

Leo Durocher was rehired for a seventh season as manager of the Cubs. The 1971 season was marked by considerable acrimony between Durocher and his players, who wanted him fired. In September, P. K. Wrigley went so far as to take out an advertisement in all four of Chicago's daily newspapers in which he criticized his players for their festering quarrel with Durocher. The manifesto was virtually without precedent. "Leo is the manager," wrote Wrigley, "and the 'Dump Durocher Clique' might as well give up. He is running the team, and if some of the players do not like it and lie down on the job, during the off-season we will see what we can do to find them happier homes." After the season ended, Wrigley wavered for several weeks, however, before deciding to retain Durocher, but his contract was renewed with an unusual clause. Hank Aguirre was hired as an "information services coach" to serve as a liaison between the acerbic Durocher and the players, and Durocher and the hostile Chicago press corps. Aguirre was in full uniform during games but had a locker in the player's clubhouse. Durocher was 66 years old and unable to change, remaining profane, irascible and inconsiderate. Controversy continued to swirl around him. Leo was relieved of his duties as Cubs manager in July 1972.

The question of the day.

How did a game involving the Cubs lead to the implication of the "Black Sox" in the 1919 World Series scandal?

Before the Cubs-Phillies game in Chicago on August 31, 1920, club President Bill Veeck, Sr. received a telegram informing him of heavy betting on the Phillies. The wire warned Veeck of rumors that the game was fixed. He replaced starting pitcher Claude Hendrix with Grover Alexander and the Cubs lost 3-0. According to some reports, Hendrix bet $5,000 on the Cubs to lose. He did not play for the rest of the season and was released in February 1921. Hendrix never played another major league game. Buck Herzog played in the game against the Phillies but was implicated as one of those involved in the fix. He was benched for the rest of the season and then released. In September the Cook County grand jury convened to investigate gambling in baseball. In addition to looking into the Cubs-Phillies game, they examined the 1919 White Sox–Reds World Series because of suspicions the White Sox may have thrown the games. There was not enough evidence to prosecute the Cubs, and the grand jury focused their attention on the White Sox. On September 28, the grand jury indicted eight White Sox players for conspiring to throw the 1919 Series. They became forever known as the "Black Sox."

Happy Birthday Rick Monday.

An outfielder with the Cubs from 1972 through 1976, Rick Monday was born on this date in 1945. On April 25, 1976, the 100th anniversary of the first game in Cubs history, Monday rescued the American flag during a 10-inning, 5-4 loss to the Dodgers in Los Angeles. Playing center field, Monday noticed two fans climbing out of the stands and running to left-center in the fourth inning. One of them was holding something under his arm. As the man unfurled his bundle and spread it on the field, Monday recognized it was the American flag. As he later recalled, "I saw they had a can of something and were pouring it over the flag. That's when I started to move." Before the two could set the flag on fire, Monday swept in, snatched it, and carried it to the bullpen. As he ran off, security personnel moved in and arrested the intruders. The crowd gave Monday a standing ovation. Overnight, Monday became a hero in the year of the nation's bicentennial and received more recognition for the flag incident than anything else he did during his 19-year playing career. The Illinois legislature proclaimed a statewide "Rick Monday Day," and he was named the grand marshal of the Flag Day parade in Chicago.

The question of the day.

How did women's hat fashions affect watching baseball 100 years ago?

During the first decade of the 1900s, women made a fashion statement by wearing enormous hats, which often caused problems at the ballpark. According to the August 28, 1908, issue of the *Chicago Journal* "a girl with a white dress and immense purple hat got behind the catcher" at the August 27 game at West Side Grounds, "and over 900 fans lost sight of the game. She stuck for seven innings, amid cries of 'A dollar for a foul tip into the purple lid,' and then left with a contemptuous glare at the wild myriads." It was not any better in Cincinnati. "Many a fan pays his 75 cents," wrote Jack Ryder in the *Cincinnati Enquirer* in 1910, "and goes home with no remembrance of anything but a mass of millinery and a few waving plumes."

The question of the day.

What was Telstar?

Today we take for granted that live televised images can be transmitted around the world in the blink of an eye, but it was not until 1962 and the launching of Telstar, the world's first communications satellite, that it was possible. The very first live sports event telecast from the United States to Europe was a small portion of a 5-3 Cubs loss to the Phillies at Wrigley Field that beamed across the Atlantic on July 23, 1962. Millions on the European continent saw Tony Taylor of the Phillies fly out to George Altman in right field. Fans at Wrigley were informed of the historic program and waved to the camera as it panned over the grandstand. In addition to the scene at Wrigley Field, Europeans were able to watch a portion of President John Kennedy's press conference and views of the New York skyline, Niagara Falls, San Francisco's Golden Gate Bridge, the U.S.-Mexican border, the Seattle World's Fair and Mt. Rushmore. The program was carried in Austria, Belgium, Denmark, England, Finland, France, Italy, Luxembourg, the Netherlands, Norway, Portugal, Spain, Sweden, Switzerland, West Germany and Yugoslavia.

23
November

On this date in 1948 . . .

Future Hall of Famer Hack Wilson died at the age of 48 from the affects of alcoholism. Despite his success on the field, Wilson died penniless. His body went unclaimed for three days because his family refused to pay for the burial. National League President Ford Frick paid $350 for the funeral. The Cubs drafted Wilson from the Toledo club in the American Association on October 9, 1925. He played for the Giants from 1923 through 1925, but the club dismissed him because his drinking and happy-go-lucky attitude did not sit well with Giants manager John McGraw. With the Cubs, Wilson developed into an immediate star. In six seasons in Chicago, he hit 190 homers, drove in 768 runs, and batted .322. In 1930, Wilson collected a major league record 191 RBIs, along with 56 home runs, which stood as the National League record until 1998. He also maintained a .356 batting average. The only two players since 1940 who have driven in as many as 160 runs are Manny Ramirez, who had 165 with the Indians in 1999, and Sammy Sosa, with 160 as a Cub in 2001. Wilson was elected to the Hall of Fame in 1979.

24
November

The question of the day.

Who holds the major league record for the longest relief appearance in a game?

Some records will never be broken. The 18⅓-inning performance by Zip Zabel of the Cubs on June 17, 1915, during a 5-4 win against the Dodgers in Chicago is one of those. Zabel entered the game for starter Bert Humphries, who left with two out in the first inning when he was hit in the hand by a line drive off Zack Wheat. Zabel pitched the rest of the game. Both teams scored in the 15th inning, the Cubs tally coming on a home run by Vic Saier. The winning run scored in the 19th on a single by Tom Fisher, who moved to second base on a sacrifice and scored on an error by Brooklyn second baseman George Cutshaw.

The question of the day.

What happened when the Cubs tried to raise their 1908 world championship pennant?

Maybe this is how the curse started. In ceremonies prior to a 3-1 win over the Dodgers on June 16, 1909, at West Side Grounds, the Cubs attempted to raise the banner emblematic of winning the 1908 World Series. There was a parade of players from both teams around the playing field, headed by a brass band, and then a march to the flagpole. Just before reaching the top of the pole, however, the rope pulley broke and the pennant blew away behind the bleachers in center field.

The question of the day.

How many Cubs have hit a home run in their first at-bat in the majors?

There have been five players in Cubs history with home runs in their first at-bats in the majors. Catcher Paul Gillespie was the first during a 4-3 loss to the Giants in New York on August 23, 1943. Gillespie also homered in his last at-bat in 1945 but finished his career with only six home runs in 205 at-bats. Right fielder Frank Ernaga homered in his first at-bat and tripled in his second during a 5-1 win over the Braves in Chicago on May 24, 1957. Ernaga ended his career with just two home runs in 43 at-bats. Catcher Cuno Barragan homered in his first plate appearance on September 1, 1961, during a 14-inning, 4-3 loss to the Giants at Wrigley Field. It proved to be Barragan's only career home run in 163 at-bats. Carmelo Martinez homered in his first official at-bat in the majors on August 22, 1983, during a 2-0 win over the Reds at Wrigley Field. Martinez appeared in 29 games and hit six homers with the Cubs before being traded to the Padres. He played nine seasons in the big leagues and hit 108 home runs. Relief pitcher Jim Bullinger also homered on the first pitch of his first at-bat during a 5-2 win over the Cardinals on June 8, 1992, in St. Louis. He finished his career in the majors in 1997 with four home runs in 165 at-bats.

27

November

The question of the day.

Who gave up Stan Musial's 3,000th career hit?

Cubs pitcher Moe Drabowsky gave up Stan Musial's 3,000th career hit on May 13, 1958, during a 5-3 Cardinals win at Wrigley Field. Musial was held out of the starting lineup so that he could collect his 3,000th hit in St. Louis, where the Cards were scheduled to play the following day. With the Cubs leading 3-1 in the sixth and a runner on second base, manager Fred Hutchinson brought Musial off the bench, and Stan delivered a run-scoring double. Drabowsky was born in Ozanna, Poland, before his family moved to the United States in 1938 and settled in Connecticut. He was a 21-year-old rookie with the Cubs in 1957 and posted a 13-15 record in 239⅔ innings. Moe never pitched that many innings again and never won as many as 13 games again, but he had a big-league career that lasted until 1972 with seven clubs, mostly as a reliever.

28

November

On this date in 1927 . . .

The Cubs traded Sparky Adams and Pete Scott to the Pirates for future Hall of Fame outfielder Kiki Cuyler. This proved to be one of the best trades in club history, as Cuyler became a fixture in Chicago for eight seasons. Cuyler was one of the top outfielders in baseball with the Pirates but was benched during the 1927 season by manager Donie Bush for objecting to move from third to second in the batting order. Cuyler hit .325 as a Cub and joined Riggs Stephenson and Hack Wilson to form one of the best outfields in major league history.

29 November

The question of the day.

Who is the youngest player to hit a home run in a Cub uniform?

Outfielder Danny Murphy became the youngest Cubs player to homer on September 13, 1960, during an 8-6 loss to the Reds. He was only 21 days past his 18th birthday. Murphy made his big-league bow as a 17-year-old on June 26, 1960. A native of Danvers, Massachusetts, Murphy signed a contract right out of high school for $125,000, at the time one of the largest bonuses ever paid to an amateur. Murphy was rushed too soon, however, and had a .171 batting average over three seasons with the Cubs. He later became a pitcher and was 4-4 with the White Sox in 1969 and 1970. Phil Cavarretta was 61 days past his 18th birthday when he hit his first home run on September 25, 1934. It happened nine days after making his major league debut in a game against the Dodgers in Brooklyn. Cavarretta was playing in his first game with the club in Chicago in his first major league start, and he hit the first pitch of his first plate appearance for a home run. The run held up for a 1-0 win over the Reds.

30 November

The question of the day.

Who is the oldest player to hit a home run for the Cubs?

Cap Anson is the oldest Cub to homer in a game at 45 years, 169 days. Anson homered twice in the first game of a double-header against the Cardinals in St. Louis, a 10-9 Chicago loss. It was his first multi-home run game since 1888. Anson was hitless in three at-bats in the second game, a 7-1 win. The two games proved to be the last two of Anson's playing career. The club released him in February 1898 after 22 years as a player and 18 as a player-manager. Anson still ranks first among Cubs in hits (3,055), batting average (.339), runs (1,719), RBIs (1,879) and doubles (528). He is second in games (2,276), second in at-bats (9,173), second in triples (124) and third in total bases (4,062).

Wrigley Hits 100

December

01 December

The question of the day.

Who was Larry Cheney?

Larry Cheney made his first major league start as a Cub on September 17, 1911, in the second game of a double-header against the Dodgers in Chicago and was the winner in a 5-0 decision. He was not around for the end of the contest, however, because he was literally knocked out of the box in the eighth inning. Zack Wheat hit a wicked line drive at Cheney's head, driving his thumb into his nose, and breaking both. The next year, he could not grip the ball tightly and changed his delivery by digging his fingernails into the ball, creating a knuckle ball delivery. Armed with the new pitch, Cheney went 26-10 as a 26-year-old rookie in 1912, tying the league lead in wins and leading it in complete games with 28. In 1913, Cheney appeared in 54 games, 36 of them starts, and compiled a 21-14 record and a league-leading 11 saves. He continued his role as the Cubs number one starter and reliever in 1914, and was 20-18 with five saves. But the dual role ruined his arm, and Cheney went into a steep decline. After 1914, his won-lost record was 48-58.

02 December

On this date in 1965 . . .

The Cubs traded Lindy McDaniel, Don Landrum and Don Rittwage to the Giants for Randy Hundley and Bill Hands. The 1965 season was the 19th in a row in which the Cubs finished in the lower half of the NL standings, and the club realized the only path to rebuilding was to trade veterans for young and promising players like Hundley and Hands in high-risk/high-reward trades. This one helped turn the sad-sack Cubs into winners during the late-1960s and early-1970s. Hundley was the Cubs starting catcher from 1966 through 1973, and Hands won 92 games with the club. Hundley also brought an end to the carousel at the catching position. From 1941 through 1965, the Cubs used 50 different men at catcher. Hundley caught 612 of the 626 games the Cubs played from 1966 through 1969. In 1968, Randy set a major league record for most games caught in a season with 160, 156 of them as a starter. His durability was due in part to becoming the first big-league catcher to adopt the one-handed catching style, in which he protected his bare hand from foul tips by placing it behind his back. Randy's son Todd played 15 seasons in the majors as a catcher, including 2001 and 2002 with the Cubs.

03
December

The question of the day.

How many times have the Cubs been in first place on June 15 or later since 1967 but failed to reach the post-season?

In seven of 12 seasons from 1967 through 1978, the Cubs were in first place on June 15 or later and failed to finish first. It has happened in three years since 1978. In 2001, the Cubs blew leads in both the division and wild-card races. The following is a list of seasons since 1967 in which the Cubs place in June or later.

Year	Pennant Race	Largest Lead	Last Day in First	Finish	GB
1967	NL	Tie	July 24	3rd	14.0
1969	NL East	8.0	September 9	2nd	8.0
1970	NL East	5.0	June 23	2nd	5.0
1973	NL East	8.5	July 22	5th	5.0
1975	NL East	4.0	June 6	5th	17.5
1977	NL East	8.5	August 6	4th	20.0
1978	NL East	3.5	June 23	3rd	11.0
1985	NL East	4.0	June 15	4th	23.5
2001	NL Central	6.0	August 17	3rd	5.0
2001	NL Wild Card	1.5	September 6	4th	4.0
2004	NL Wild Card	1.5	September 28	3rd	3.0

Happy Birthday Lee Smith.

Born on this date in 1957, Lee Smith recorded a club-record 180 saves for the Cubs from 1980 through 1987. He should have had a few hundred more in Chicago, but general manager Jim Frey was swindled in a trade on December 8, 1987, which sent Smith to the Red Sox for Al Nipper and Calvin Schiraldi. Smith had another eight seasons ahead of him as one of the top closers in the game. Neither Nipper nor Schiraldi were of any help to the Cubs. Without Smith, the Cubs bullpen blew 27 saves in 56 chances in 1988. Lee finished his career with 478 saves, which was the major league record until Trevor Hoffman passed him in 2006.

On this date in 1988 . . .

The Cubs traded Rafael Palmeiro, Jamie Moyer and Drew Hall to the Rangers for Mitch Williams, Paul Kilgus, Steve Wilson, Curtis Wilkerson, Luis Benitez and Pablo Delgado. Cubs fans are still harping about the 1964 Lou Brock trade, but this one was far worse. Palmeiro posted outstanding numbers throughout his career. He was second in the NL in batting average in 1988, with an average of .307, although he had not yet developed his power stroke, clubbing just eight home runs. The Cubs traded him, in part, because they did not believe he had the power required of a left fielder or a first baseman and was too slow to effectively play in the outfield. After the trade, Palmeiro collected 2,763 hits and 544 home runs. Moyer was still good enough in 2003 to post a 21-7 record with the Mariners. In 2008, he was an effective member of the Phillies rotation at the age of 45. Since leaving the Cubs, he has won over 200 games.

06 December

Happy Birthday Jocko Conlan.

Umpire Jocko Conlan, born on this date in Chicago in 1899, helped cause a commotion at Wrigley Field during a game against the Braves on August 26, 1948. The Braves led 1-0 in the third inning of the second game of a double-header on a 95-degree day when Conlan credited Phil Cavarretta with a ground-rule double instead of an inside-the-park home run. Cavarretta's drive bounced into the ivy, stuck there for about 10 seconds and then fell to the ground. Boston left fielder Jeff Heath did not see the ball drop and kept looking for it in the ivy when it was actually by his foot. The ball was in full view of the fans. Play was held up for about 20 minutes as the field was showered with straw hats, hot dog wrappers, fruit and bottles. Conlan got in on the excitement as well, chewing out a Chicago police officer for not taking action. At one point, there were several hundred fans on the field. When order was restored, Andy Pafko was intentionally walked, setting off another barrage of debris, before Peanuts Lowrey cleared the bases with a triple that Heath had to chase into the left-field corner. The Cubs went on to win the contest 5-2.

07 December

The question of the day.

How did World War II stop a plan to install lights at Wrigley Field?

Were it not for the Japanese attack on Pearl Harbor on December 7, 1941, the first Cubs night game at Wrigley Field would have taken place in 1942, not 1988. By the end of the 1941 season, nine of the 16 big-league clubs were playing home games under the lights. Cubs owner P. K. Wrigley had been intrigued by playing at night but was afraid the light towers would destroy the park-like setting of his beloved Wrigley Field. He hated the "freight yard" look that 1940s-era light towers imposed on a ballpark. Wrigley decided to install lights for the 1942 season because of declining attendance. After a peak of 1,485,166 in 1929, the club drew only 545,159 in 1941. He bought the lighting equipment under an assumed name at a cost of $185,000 and secretly stored it beneath the Wrigley Field grandstand. Work was to have begun on December 8, 1941. It was on that day that the United States declared war on Japan in the wake of the Pearl Harbor attack. With the country suddenly at war, Wrigley called the War Department and offered the 165 tons of steel, 35,000 feet of copper wire and aluminum deflectors for use in one of the many new military facilities being built across the country.

The question of the day.

What Reds pitcher beat the Cubs with a triple play after only throwing on pitch?

In Cincinnati on July 27, 1930, Reds pitcher Ken Ash earned all three outs and a victory on one pitch. It was one of the strangest triple plays ever as all three outs came with the tag of a runner. Ash took the mound in relief of Larry Benton with no one out in the sixth inning, Cubs base runners Hack Wilson on third, Danny Taylor on first and the Reds trailing 3-2. On Ash's first pitch, Charlie Grimm hit a routine grounder to second baseman Hod Ford, who saw Wilson breaking for the plate. After Ford's throw to catcher Clyde Sukeforth, Wilson was retired in a rundown between Sukeforth and third baseman Tony Cuccinello. Grimm tried reaching second during the rundown, only to find Taylor on the bag. Grimm quickly retreated to first base and was out on a toss from Sukeforth to first baseman Joe Stripp. Taylor tried to advance to third during the Grimm putout but was retired on a Stripp-to-Cuccinello throw to complete the unusual triple play. Ash was lifted for a pinch-hitter in the bottom of the sixth as the Reds scored four times and held on for a 6-5 win.

On this date in 1992 . . .

Greg Maddux signed a contract as a free agent with the Braves. Maddux proved to be huge loss, of course. The Cubs should have been able to sign him because Maddux wanted to remain in Chicago, but the star pitcher became angry because general manager Larry Himes took a hard line during contract negotiations. Maddux signed with the Braves for $28 million over five years. He would have been a bargain at twice the price. It is difficult to believe the Cubs thought they could win without him. From 1988 through 1992, Maddux was 95-75, a winning percentage of .559. The rest of the staff was 307-331 (.481). With the Braves, Maddux had a record of 194-88, led the NL in ERA four times and won three Cy Young Awards.

The question of the day.

Why did Cubs manager Don Zimmer promise to swim across Lake Michigan?

Don Zimmer promised to swim across Lake Michigan if Greg Maddux beat the Padres at Wrigley Field on July 18, 1990. Maddux entered the game with 13 consecutive starts since May 5 without a victory. He lost eight games and had five no decisions while compiling an ERA of 6.15. Maddux won the game 4-2. Zimmer showed up at the post-game press interview wearing sunglasses, a life jacket and a buoy strapped around his leg. Within 48 hours, Zimmer was inundated with flotation devices. As to swimming the 60 miles across the lake, Zimmer said, "I didn't think anyone would take me seriously. I swim like a rock."

On this date in 1917 . . .

The Cubs sent Mike Prendergast, Pickles Dillhoefer and $60,000 to the Phillies for Grover Alexander and Bill Killefer. The $60,000 price was the largest ever paid for a player up to that time. Alexander had been in the majors seven years and had a record of 190-88. The Phillies let him go because it was likely that Alexander would be drafted by the Army before the start of the 1918 season because of World War I, and owner Bill Baker believed that Alexander's $12,000 salary was too much to pay in a wartime economy. Cubs owner Charles Weeghman felt that Alexander was just the player to bring the Cubs a pennant and was willing to spend the money in spite of the war. Weeghman was losing the attendance war in Chicago to Charles Comiskey, as the White Sox drew 684,521 fans in 1917 to 360,218 for the Cubs. Alexander was of little help to the Cubs in 1918, as he was drafted after pitching just three games. But he returned in 1919 and remained with the club until 1926. Although he never reached the peak level he enjoyed with the Phillies, Alexander was an excellent addition. As a Cub, he had a record of 128-83.

12
December

On this date in 1903 . . .

The Cubs traded Jack Taylor and Larry McLean to the Cardinals for Mordecai "Three Fingers" Brown and Jack O'Neil. The Cubs traded their top starter in Taylor for the unproven Brown, but this turned out to be one of the greatest deals in the history of the franchise. Taylor was traded because of unsubstantiated charges that he threw games to the White Sox during the 1903 City Series. At the time of the trade, Mordecai Centennial "Three Finger" Brown was 27 years old and had won only nine big-league games. Once in Chicago, he became a star. He played for the club from 1904 through 1912 and again in 1916 with a 188-85 record. Among Cubs hurlers he ranks second in wins, second in winning percentage (.689), first in shutouts (49), first in ERA (1.80), fourth in complete games (206), fifth in innings (2,329) and ninth in games (346). Brown was elected to the Hall of Fame in 1949. His nickname was the result of an accident he suffered at age seven: he stuck his right hand into a corn chopper, whcih cutt off half of the right index finger. The thumb and middle finger were badly damaged. A few weeks later he fell while chasing a hog and further mangled the hand, breaking the third and fourth fingers. As they healed, each finger bent and twisted unnaturally. The disfigured hand gave Brown a unique grip, which aided his pitching.

13
December

Happy Birthday Ferguson Jenkins.

Hall of Famer Ferguson Jenkins was born on this date in 1942 in Chatham, Ontario, Canada. He was acquired in a trade on April 21, 1966, that sent veteran pitchers Larry Jackson and Bob Buhl for unproven youngsters Jenkins, Adolpho Phillips and John Herrnstein. Jenkins was not considered to be the key player in the trade, however. Phillips was the athlete the Cubs most coveted. But it was the success of Jenkins who made the trade one of the best in club history. As a Cub, he was 167-132 and won 20 or more games six consecutive seasons from 1967 through 1972. Among Cubs pitchers, Jenkins is fifth all-time in victories and also ranks first in strikeouts (2,038), first in games started (347), fifth in complete games (154), fourth in shutouts (29) and third in innings (2,673⅓). The only Cubs hurlers since 1900 with a better career in Chicago than Jenkins are Three Finger Brown and Charlie Root, and Jenkins is head and shoulders above anyone who has pitched for the club since 1940. Jenkins was elected to the Hall of Fame in 1991.

On this date in 1948 . . .

The Cubs traded Eddie Waitkus and Hank Borowy to the Phillies for Dutch Leonard and Monk Dubiel. It turned out to be a fateful deal for Waitkus. On June 14, 1949, while on a road trip with the Phillies to Chicago, he was shot with a .22-caliber rifle in Room 1279A of the Edgewater Beach Hotel by 19-year-old Ruth Steinhagen. The teenager became obsessed with Waitkus while he played for the Cubs and created a shrine dedicated to the ballplayer in her bedroom. Waitkus was taken to Illinois Masonic Hospital with a bullet in the muscles near his spine and a collapsed right lung. He missed the remainder of the 1949 season, but returned to play 154 games in 1950. Waitkus refused to press charges, and Steinhagen was confined to a mental institution. She was released in April 1952.

On this date in 1979 . . .

Stan Hack, who played third base for the Cubs from 1932 through 1947, died. He also managed the club from 1954 through 1956. Among Cubs, he is the all-time leader in walks with 1,092 and also ranks seventh in games (1,938), sixth in at-bats (7,278), sixth in hits (2,193), seventh in runs (1,239), seventh in doubles (363), ninth in triples (91) and 10th in total bases (2,889). Hack was extremely popular with the fans for his pleasant and outgoing disposition. In 1935, 21-year-old Bill Veeck, working in the Cubs front office, used Hack's perpetual smile as a promotional gimmick by selling "Smile With Stan Hack" mirrors at Wrigley Field. The National League put a stop to the practice when fans in the bleachers were using the mirrors to reflect the sun in the eyes of opposing batters.

16 December

Happy Birthday Adolpho Phillips.

A center fielder with the Cubs from 1966 through 1969, Adolpho Phillips was born on this date in 1941. On June 11, 1967, he became one of two players in Cubs history to hit four homers in a double-header. The other was Bill Nicholson in 1944. Phillips accomplished his feat with one in the first game and three in the second as the Cubs swept the Mets 5-3 and 18-10 at Wrigley Field. Phillips hit a solo homer in the first tilt. Following his first at-bat in game two, Adolpho attempted to steal home and was tagged in the head by New York catcher Hawk Taylor. Phillips was knocked dizzy but stayed in the game. In his next three plate appearances, Phillips went deep, connecting off Nick Willhite in the third inning with two runners on base, hitting a two-run shot off Chuck Estrada in the fifth and belting a solo shot against Don Shaw in the sixth. Phillips added a seventh run batted in with a single in the eighth. The Cubs and Mets tied for a National League-record 11 home runs in the game, seven of them by the Cubs, a team record. Phillips was a favorite of the Bleacher Bums, who loved to shout "Ole! Adolpho Ole!" while giving him a standing ovation after a great play, but he proved to be a disappointment after being called the "Next Willie Mays" by Leo Durocher.

17 December

On this date in 1933 . . .

The first scheduled championship game since the NFL's founding in 1920 took place at Wrigley Field in 1933. The game pitted the champions of the NFL's two divisions against one another, with the mighty Bears from the West taking on the Beasts from the East, the New York Giants. The Bears scored the winning touchdown with less than 2 minutes to go in the fourth quarter, capping a 23–21 victory. An interesting footnote: This was the second consecutive title for the Chicago Bears. In 1932, the title game was set to be played at Wrigley Field, but because of severe blizzards and sub-zero wind chill, the game was moved indoors to Chicago Stadium.

18
December

The question of the day.

How did a change in managers help the Cubs win the pennant in 1932 and 1938?

The Cubs changed managers on August 2, 1932, replacing Rogers Hornsby with Charlie Grimm. At the time, the Cubs were 53-46 and five games behind the Pirates. There were reports of internal strife over Hornsby's martinet methods at the time of his dismissal. In addition, he owed his players several thousand dollars in gambling debts, including $1,115 to Woody English. The debts were paid when the club deducted money from Hornsby's remaining paychecks. Under the easygoing Grimm, the Cubs won 28 of their first 34 games, had a record of 37-18 over the remainder of the season and won the NL pennant. During the stretch run, the Cubs won 14 games in a row. In Grimm's first 32 days as manager, the Cubs overcame a five-game deficit to take a seven-game lead in the NL race. Grimm was fired on July 20, 1938, and replaced with starting catcher Gabby Hartnett. The Cubs had a 45-36 record at the time of the move. P. K. Wrigley believed that Grimm was too easy on the players and wanted the tougher and gruffer Hartnett in charge. The Cubs went on to win the NL pennant again after changing managers in mid-season.

19
December

On this date in 1996 . . .

Luis Gonzalez signed a contract with the Astros as a free agent. Gonzalez did not look like a huge loss. He was 29 years old, sported a .270 lifetime batting average and had never hit more than 15 homers in a season. He was considered to be no more than a platoon outfielder who could not hit lefties. In 1999, he ended up with the Arizona Diamondbacks, and in a completely unexpected development, Gonzalez became one of the most feared hitters in the game. From 1999 through 2003, he batted .314 and averaged 34 homers and 115 RBIs a season while the Cubs struggled to find a consistent left fielder to team with Sammy Sosa. Imagine this duo playing the corner outfield positions for the Cubs. In 2001, Sosa hit 64 homers and Gonzalez clubbed 57. One can also ponder the fact that ex-Cub Rafael Palmeiro hit 47 homers that season for the Rangers.

Happy Birthday Gabby Hartnett.

A catcher with the Cubs from 1922 through 1940 and a Hall of Famer, Gabby Hartnett was born on this date in 1900. On September 28, 1938, he provided what is arguably the greatest moment in Cubs history. In the thickening gloom of Wrigley Field, Hartnett hit a walk-off home run to defeat the Pirates 6-5. The win was the ninth in a row for the Cubs and put the club into first place, a half-game ahead of Pittsburgh. The Pirates broke a 3-3 tie with two runs in the eighth inning, but the Cubs scored twice in their half of the inning, evening the score. With two out and no one on base, Ripper Collins hit a single, Billy Jurges walked, Tony Lazzeri pinch-hit for a double to score Collins and Billy Herman singled to bring across the tying run. Hartnett stepped to the plate against Pirate reliever Mace Brown with two out in the ninth and the score still 5-5. If Hartnett was retired, the umpires planned to call the game on account of darkness. Hartnett's game-winning drive came on a 0-2 pitch at 5:37 p.m. While circling the bases, Hartnett had to fight his way through a delirious mob of fans that surged onto the field. Three days later, the Cubs clinched the NL pennant. The home run has gone down in Cubs lore as the "Homer in the Gloamin.'"

On this date in 1941. . .

As you've noticed by now, there's little on-field baseball action during the winter, but that doesn't mean Wrigley went dark for the season—it just switched up the sports. The 1941 National Football League Championship game played at Wrigley was the ninth-annual championship game. The game was played two weeks after Pearl Harbor, which in turn led to the smallest crowd ever to see an NFL title game (a hair over 13,000).

Once again, it was the Bears versus the New York Giants. The Bears triumphed 37–9, and in the process became the first team since the NFL adopted the championship game in 1933 to win back-to-back titles. According to ESPN, Ray "Scooter" McLean drop-kicked the extra point on the last touchdown. This would be the last drop-kick in the NFL until Doug Flutie of the New England Patriots kicked one in the last game of the season in 2005.

Coincidentally, the Bears had won the championship both in 1932 and 1933, but the first game was prior to the standardized Eastern Division–Western Division champions.

22
December

The question of the day.
What were the only two winning seasons by the Cubs from 1973 through 1992?

Over a 20-year span from 1973 through 1992, the Cubs won more than they lost only in 1984 and 1989. Oddly, both resulted in Eastern Division championships. The Cubs were 96-65 in 1984 and won the division by 6½ games. The .596 winning percentage is the best of any Wrigley Field team since 1945. In 1989, the Cubs compiled a record of 93-69 and won the NL East by six games. Stranger still, both pennant-winning years came after horrible spring training records. The Cubs were 7-20 in 1984 and 9-23 in 1989.

23
December

The question of the day.
When was the last time the Cubs compiled a winning percentage of .550 or better in back-to-back seasons?

To compose a winning percentage of .550 or better over the course of a 162-game schedule, a team needs to win 90 games. It has been over 70 years since the Cubs have been .550 or better in consecutive seasons. In 1937, the club was 93-61 (.604). In 1938, the Cubs were 89-63 (.586). Of the 26 teams in existence since at least 1977, all have accomplished the feat at least once except the Padres. Established in 1969, San Diego has yet to post winning percentages of .550 or better two years in a row.

The question of the day.

Who is the only pitcher in major league history to give up hits to the first seven batters he faced in a game?

Bill Bonham is the only pitcher in history to give up hits to the first seven batters he faced in a start. He did it with the Cubs against the Phillies on August 5, 1975, in Philadelphia. Bonham gave up singles to Dave Cash and Larry Bowa, a homer to Garry Maddox, a single to Greg Luzinski, doubles to Jay Johnstone and Tim Hutton and a homer to Mike Schmidt before being lifted in favor of Ken Crosby. The Phillies tied a major league record for most consecutive hits at the start of a game with eight when Johnny Oates singled off Crosby. The Cubs lost 13-5. In his next start, on August 11, Bonham retired the first 12 batters he faced and beat the Braves 9-1 in Atlanta with a complete game five-hitter.

The question of the day.

Who is the only pitcher to throw a perfect game against the Cubs?

Sandy Koufax pitched a perfect game for the Dodgers, and Bob Hendley of the Cubs allowed only one hit in a 1-0 Los Angeles win at Dodger Stadium on September 9, 1965. It is the only major league game in history of nine innings or more in which both teams combined for only one hit. Lou Johnson was the only batter to reach base, collecting a walk and a double. Koufax struck out 14 batters. Hendley had a perfect game until the fifth inning, when the Dodgers scored without a hit. Johnson walked, was sacrificed to second, stole third, and continued home on catcher Chris Krug's high throw. Johnson picked up the only hit of the game with a double in the seventh. Koufax struck out the last six men he faced, fanning Ron Santo, Ernie Banks and Byron Browne in the eighth and Krug, Joey Amalfitano and Harvey Kuenn in the ninth. Through the 2008 season, no one since Koufax has thrown a no-hitter against the Cubs. The Cubs lineup included Browne and Don Young, both making their major league debuts. Krug was named Chris by his parents because he was born on Christmas Day. He also wore uniform number 25 because of his birth on December 25.

On this date in 1943 . . .

Wrigley Field was the site of the 1943 NFL championship game, in which the Bears battled another perennial nemesis, the Washington Redskins. The game pitted two great quarterbacks against one another: Sid Luckman guided the Bears, Sammy Baugh the Redskins. Chicago's win marked the franchise's third championship in four seasons, its fourth since the institution of the championship game in 1933, and its sixth since the NFL was formed in 1921. It would be another two decades before another title was won by the Bears—once again at Wrigley.

On this date in 1932 . . .

Pop Schriver, a catcher with the Cubs from 1891 through 1894, died. Schriver pulled off a feat on August 26, 1894, by catching a ball dropped some 500 feet from the top of the Washington Monument. Baseball players visiting Washington were immediately intrigued by the notion of whether it was possible to catch a ball dropped from the top of the shaft. Many players tried and failed to make such a catch, among them Paul Hines, Pop Snyder, Hardy Richardson and future Hall of Famer Buck Ewing. It was generally believed it was beyond any man's power to catch a ball from such a great height. Furthermore, many argued that anyone who would get his hands on the ball would be seriously injured, if not killed. Pop Schriver was the first to successfully complete the task. A party of five Cubs players went to the observation platform with a supply of baseballs. Schriver let the first one fall to the ground to gauge the speed at which the ball traveled. He caught the second one cleanly to the applause of the spectators who had gathered to watch the event. Schriver did not get a chance to repeat the act, because the police officer assigned to guard the monument threatened arrest if the players continued.

The question of the day.

What injury did Ron Santo suffer during his 28-game hitting streak in 1966?

In the plate appearance after extending his streak to 26 games, Santo suffered a double fracture of the cheekbone when hit by a pitch from Jack Fisher of the Mets in the fourth inning of a 7-0 win in the first game of a double-header at Wrigley Field. The Cubs were engaged in a beam-ball war when Santo was hit. Earlier, Fisher put Adolpho Phillips out of the game by hitting him on the arm, and Cubs pitcher Curt Simmons retaliated by plunking Ron Hunt. Fisher turned around and threw at Santo. Cubs manager Leo Durocher and Mets skipper Wes Westrum nearly came to blows over the incident. Westrum, who played for Durocher for eight seasons when Leo was manager of the Giants, had to be forcibly restrained by the umpires. Santo submitted to surgery the following day to correct displacement by wiring the cheekbone. He returned to the lineup on July 4 and hit in both games of a double-header against the Pirates to extend his streak to 28 games, the third longest in club history.

On this date in 1963 . . .

In 1963, yet again it was the Bears versus the New York Giants for the NFL championship at Wrigley. NFL Commissioner Pete Rozelle asked George Halas to move the game to Soldier Field for increased seating capacity, plus lights just in case the sun were to set during the game. Halas refused. Rozelle pushed the starting time up almost an hour, with the opening whistle sounding 5 minutes past noon. The championship was also played in frigid temps—at game time, the mercury hovered between 9 and 11 degrees Fahrenheit. The temperature almost mirrored the final score: 14–10. Even though the rival AFL was still in its infancy, it posed enough of a threat that the NFL felt it had to reaffirm its prominence. As the final minute ticked off, WGN radio broadcaster Jack Quinlan drew the line in the sand for the upstart league when he announced, "The Chicago Bears are world's champions of professional football!" It would be Wrigley's final sporting championship. For the Bears, it would take another two decades (22 years, to be precise) and 15 years playing at Soldier Field before they would win another championship. Wrigley is one of only two stadiums to host at least five World Series and five NFL championship games (the other is the Polo Grounds in New York City, in operation from 1911 to 1963).

30
December

The question of the day.

What three future members of the Pro Football Hall of Fame played in the same baseball game at Wrigley Field?

Three future members of the Pro Football Hall of Fame appeared in an 8-5 Cubs loss to the Reds at Wrigley Field (then known as Weeghman Park) on July 2, 1917. Jim Thorpe and Greasy Neale played for the Reds, and Paddy Driscoll started at second base for the Cubs. Thorpe and Driscoll were both pioneers in the NFL, which was formed in 1920. Neale earned his Hall of Fame plaque as a coach with the Philadelphia Eagles during the 1940s.

31
December

Happy Birthday King Kelly.

King Kelly was born on this date in 1857. Colorful, versatile, innovative and immensely talented, Kelly played for the Cubs from 1880 through 1886. He was perhaps the greatest player of the 19th century. While in Chicago, Kelly led the NL three times in runs scored, twice in games played, twice in doubles, twice in on-base percentage and once in batting average. During his major league career, Kelly played all nine positions. He was also a first-class "man about town" who frustrated management with his drunken off-the-field escapades. In 1886, he hit .388 and scored 155 runs in 118 games but was sold to Boston after the season was over for the then-record price of $10,000 because the Cubs grew tired of his insubordination. Kelly was only 36 when he died of pneumonia in 1894. He was elected to the Hall of Fame in 1945.

About the Author

John Snyder has a master's degree in history from the University of Cincinnati and a passion for baseball. He has authored more than fifteen books on baseball, soccer, hockey, tennis, football, basketball, and travel and lives in Cincinnati.